THE
COMPLETE
SCHOOL VERSE

Dedication
This book is for Henry and Sophie,
with love

THE COMPLETE SCHOOL VERSE

Chosen by Jennifer Curry

Illustrated by Graham Thompson

RED FOX

A Red Fox Book
Published by Random House Children's Books
20 Vauxhall Bridge Road, London SW1V 2SA

A division of Random House UK Ltd

London Melbourne Sydney Auckland
Johannesburg and agencies throughout
the world

The Beaver Book of School Verse
First published 1981
© Copyright in this collection Jennifer Curry 1981
© Copyright illustrations Century Hutchinson Ltd 1984

More School Verse
First published 1986
© Copyright in this collection Jennifer and Graeme Curry 1986
© Copyright illustrations Century Hutchinson Ltd 1986

Red Fox edition 1991

This revised Red Fox edition 1998

13 15 17 19 20 18 16 14

Typeset in Bembo
by JH Graphics Ltd, Reading

Printed and bound in Great Britain by
Cox & Wyman Ltd, Reading, Berkshire

Papers used by Random House UK Limited
are natural, recyclable products made from wood grown in
sustainable forests. The manufacturing processes conform to
the environmental regulations of the country of origin.

RANDOM HOUSE UK Limited Reg. No. 954009

ISBN 0 09 991790 4

Contents

Author's Acknowledgements

Very many people have helped me to gather together the poems in this book — a lot of friends, teachers, parents and children, especially children. I would like to thank them all, but particularly, my assistant, *Graeme Curry*, for his imagination, hard work and everlasting fund of good ideas; and also *June Shirfield* and the children in her class at Downton Primary School; *Greta Pike*; *Sandy Mason*; the *Salisbury Times and Journal*; *St Edmund's Arts Centre Writers' Workshop*; *the Director, Wiltshire Library and Museum Service*; *the library of ILEA's Centre for Language in Primary Education*; and the many *Beaver Bulletin Readers* who sent in their favourite school rhymes.

Our School

I go to Weld Park Primary,
It's near the Underpass
And five blocks past the Cemetery
And two roads past the Gas
Works with the big tower that smells so bad
    me and me mates put our hankies over our
        faces and pretend we're being attacked
            by poison gas . . . and that.

There's this playground with lines for rounders,
And cricket stumps chalked on the wall,
And kids with their coats for goalposts
Booting a tennis ball
Around all over the place and shoutin' and arguin'
    about offside and they always kick it over
        the garden wall next door and she
           goes potty and tells our head teacher
           and he gets right ratty with
              everybody and stops us playin'
              football . . .
                . . . and everything.

We have this rule at our school
You've to wait till the whistle blows
And you can't go in till you hear it
Not even if it snows
And your wellies get filled with water and your socks
    go all soggy and start slipping down your legs
        and your hands get so cold they go all
           crumpled and you can't undo
             the buttons of your mac when
              you do get inside . . .
               . . . it's true.

The best thing is our classroom.
When it's fine you can see right far,
Past the Catholic Cathedral
Right to the Morris Car
Works where me Dad works as a fitter and sets off
    right early every morning in these overalls
        with his snap in this sandwich box and
            a flask of tea and always moanin'
                about the money . . . honest.

In Hall we pray for brotherly love
And sing hymns that are ever so long
And the Head shouts at Linda Nutter
Who's always doing wrong.
She can't keep out of trouble because
    she's always talkin'
        she can't stop our teacher says she
            must have been injected with
                a gramophone needle she talks
                    so much and
that made me laugh once
not any more though I've heard it
    too often . . . teachers!

Loving your enemy sounds all right
Until you open your eyes
And you're standing next to Nolan
Who's always telling lies
About me and getting me into trouble and about
    three times a week I fight him after school
        it's like a habit I've got
            but I can't love him even though
                I screw my eyes up real hard and try like
                mad, but if it wasn't him it
                    would be somebody else
                    I mean
                    you've got to have enemies . . .
                        . . . haven't you?

We sing 'O to be a pilgrim'
And think about God and heaven
And then we're told the football team lost
By thirteen goals to seven
But that's not bad because St Xavier's don't half have
    big lads in their team and last time we played
        they beat us eighteen one and this time
            we got seven goals . . .
                . . . didn't we?

Then we have our lessons,
We have Science and English and Maths,
Except on Wednesday morning
When our class goes to the baths
And it's not half cold and Peter Bradberry's
    fingers went all wrinkled and blue last week
        and I said, 'You're goin' to die, man'
            but he pushed me under the water and I had to
            hold my breath for fifteen minutes.
                But he's still alive though . . .
                    . . . he is.

Friday's my favourite day though,
We have Art all afternoon
And I never care what happens
'Cos I know it's home-time soon
And I'm free for two whole days but I think
    sometimes it wouldn't be half so good
        having this weekend if we didn't have five
            days
                of
                    school
                        in
                            between—
Would it?

Gareth Owen

GOING TO SCHOOL

Meet-on-the-Road

'Now, pray, where are you going?' said
                    Meet-on-the-Road.
'To school, sir, to school, sir,' said
                    Child-as-it-Stood.

'What have you in your basket, child?' said
                    Meet-on-the-Road.
'My dinner, sir, my dinner, sir,' said
                    Child-as-it-Stood.

'What have you for dinner, child?' said
                    Meet-on-the-Road.
'Some pudding, sir, some pudding, sir,' said
                    Child-as-it-Stood.

'Oh, then, I pray, give me a share,' said
                    Meet-on-the-Road.
'I've little enough for myself, sir,' said
                    Child-as-it-Stood.

'What have you got that cloak on for?' said
                    Meet-on-the-Road.
'To keep the wind and cold from me,' said
                    Child-as-it-Stood.

'I wish the wind would blow through you,' said
                    Meet-on-the-Road.
'Oh, what a wish!' What a wish!' said
                    Child-as-it-Stood.

'Pray, what are those bells ringing for?' said
                          Meet-on-the-Road.
'To ring bad spirits home again,' said
                          Child-as-it-Stood.

'Oh, then I must be going, child!' said
                          Meet-on-the-Road.
'So fare you well, so fare you well,' said
                          Child-as-it-Stood.

Anon

Going to School in the Country

A long walk,
two miles or more,
up hill and down, before
I get to the school gate;
I do not stop and talk
to anyone on the way,
and I am never late.
At eight o'clock today
I passed by Gunter's farm,
the men were making hay,
and then I met a herd of cows
lumbering along;
they meant no harm,
and over the fields where Gunter ploughs
each spring, a lark rose up in song;
at the end of the tall–hedged lane,
two cottages and a rick,
and there I peeled a hazel stick;
at half past nine was there,
beating a shower of rain,
ready for Miss Jones and morning prayer.

Leonard Clark

Going to School in Town

A long walk,
half a mile or more,
over four noisy roads, before
I reach the high school wall,
covered with pictures in chalk,
and hear the playground bell call
us into our lines.
I go past twenty shops, a shellfish stall,
and through a smelly tunnel where
the sun never shines,
and then across the square,
around a corner by the old King's Head
and there must wait,
do what my teacher said,
for the green light to say
that I can cross the road;
bus after bus every day
and lorries each with a different load.
And then I am
dodging the factory where they make jam,
and at last run into school there,
ready for Mr Smith and morning prayer.

Leonard Clark

The Lollipop Lady

The Lollipop Lady is not
as tall as the lollipop
but she shines in the wet.
Some days I forget
about her, and stop
with a skid in a puddle
and there is her red and white bubble
all of a sudden, twice.
The Lollipop Lady is nice;
she sorts out the muddle
and holds my hand
and stops the cars with her magic wand
so I can walk, where there aren't any stripes,
past huge big lorries and motor bikes
which roar and shake and
smoke like dragons; but all of them wait
for the Lollipop Lady's wave –
for the children. When she
smiles and nods at me
I can cross the road. If I'm as brave
as her when I grow up, *I* could be
a shining Lollipop Lady.

Jane Whittle

Marbles in my Pocket

Marbles in my pocket!
Winter-time's begun!
Marbles in my pocket
That rattle when I run!

Heavy in my pocket
On the way to school;
Smooth against my fingers,
Round and hard and cool;

Marbles in my pocket,
Blue and green and red,
And some are yellow-golden,
And some are brown instead.

Marbles in the playground,
Big and little ring –
Oh, I like playing marbles,
But that's a different thing.

Marbles in my pocket,
Smooth within my hand,
That's the part that's nicest;
Do you understand?

Marbles in my pocket
To rattle when I run!
For winter days are here again,
And marble-time's begun!

Lydia Pender

I've Got an Apple Ready

My hair's tightly plaited;
I've a bright blue bow;
I don't want my breakfast,
And now I must go.

My satchel's on my shoulder;
Nothing's out of place;
And I've got an apple ready,
Just in case.

So it's 'Goodbye, Mother!'
And off down the street!
Briskly at first
On pit-a-pat feet,

But slow and more slow
As I reach the tarred
Trackway that runs
By Hodson's Yard;

For it's there sometimes
Bill Craddock waits for me
To snatch off my beret
And throw it in a tree.

Bill Craddock is leaning
On Hodson's rails;
Bill with thin hands
And dirty nails;

Bill with a front tooth
Broken and bad;
His dark eyes cruel,
And somewhat sad.

Often there are workmen,
And then he doesn't dare;
But this morning I feel
He'll be there.

At the corner he will pounce . . .
But quickly I'll say
'Hallo, Bill, have an apple!' –
In an ordinary way.

I'll push it in his hand
And walk right on;
And when I'm round the corner
I'll run.

John Walsh

Bus to School

Rounding a corner
It comes to stay.
Quick. Grab the rail!
Now we're off on our way . . .

Here in the bus though
There's plenty to see:
Boys full of talk about
Last night's T.V.
Girls with their violins,
Armfuls of twigs
And flowers for the teacher.
Bartlett and Biggs
Conductor who chats with them,
Jokes about cricket;
Machine that flicks out
A white ribbon of ticket . . .

Conductor now waiting,
Firm as a rock,
For Billy, whose penny's
Slid down his sock,
Conductor frowning,
With finger on handle:
Poor Billy blushes,
Undoes his sandal . . .
'Hold very tight, please!
Any more fares?'
Whistling conductor
Goes clumping upstairs . . .

Boots up above, now!
Boys coming down! . . .
Over the hump bridge
And into the town.

John Walsh

The School Bus Breaks Down

As up the hill the school bus goes,
Just listen how it puffs and blows.
It coughs and splutters as it tries
To drag its body up the rise,
Until at last it wearies out
And stops. Then with a joyful shout
The children jump down to the ground
And laugh and skip and run around.

'We'll all be late for school! Hurray!
It's not our fault!' they chant with glee.
'Sit down. We'll soon be on our way!'
The driver roars. 'Don't crowd round me!'

He takes a crank, and twirls it round.
The boys and girls soon hear the sound
Of engines turning. In they hop.
And with another start and stop
The bus moves off. With downcast face
Each child sits in his normal place.
'School after all!' they sadly say.
'I thought we might have missed today!'

Phyllis Telfer and Hermea Goodman

The Schoolboy

I love to rise in a summer morn
When the birds sing on every tree;
The distant huntsman winds his horn,
And the sky-lark sings with me.
O! what sweet company.

But to go to school in a summer morn,
O! it drives all joy away;
Under a cruel eye outworn,
The little ones spend the day
In sighing and dismay.

Ah! then at times I drooping sit,
And spend many an anxious hour,
Nor in my book can I take delight,
Nor sit in learning's bower,
Worn thro' with the dreary shower.

How can the bird that is born for joy
Sit in a cage and sing?
How can a child, when fears annoy,
But droop his tender wing,
And forget his youthful spring?

William Blake

First Day at School

A millionbillionwillion miles from home
Waiting for the bell to go. (To go where?)
Why are they all so big, other children?
So noisy? So much at home they
must have been born in uniform.
Lived all their lives in playgrounds.
Spent the years inventing games
that don't let me in. Games
that are rough, that swallow you up.

And the railings.
All around, the railings.
Are they to keep out wolves and monsters?
Things that carry off and eat children?
Things you don't take sweets from?
Perhaps they're to stop us getting out
Running away from the lessins. Lessin.
What does a lessin look like?
Sounds small and slimy.
They keep them in glassrooms.
Whole rooms made out of glass. Imagine.

I wish I could remember my name
Mummy said it would come in useful.
Like wellies. When there's puddles.
Yellowwellies. I wish she was here.
I think my name is sewn on somewhere
Perhaps the teacher will read it for me.
Tea'cher. The one who makes the tea.

Roger McGough

School Bell

Nine–o'Clock Bell!
Nine–o'Clock Bell!
All the small children and big ones as well,
Pulling their stockings up, snatching their hats,
Cheeking and grumbling and giving back–chats,
Laughing and quarrelling, dropping their things,
These at a snail's pace and those upon wings,
Lagging behind a bit, running ahead,
Waiting at corners for lights to turn red,
Some of them scurrying,
Others not worrying,
Carelessly trudging or anxiously hurrying,
All through the streets they are coming pell–mell
At the Nine–o'Clock
      Nine–o'Clock
      Nine–o'Clock
          Bell!

Eleanor Farjeon

The New Boy

Slowly he trundles into school clinging tightly to his
                    mother's hand,
Crying a little.
He holds his mother's dress shyly.
Children stand like giants to him when he is just a
                    scared mouse.
In the cloakroom the giants push around him
To reach their pegs.
He feels like a football.

Karen Aldous (aged 7)

IN THE CLASSROOM

In Hall

'All things bright and beautiful . . .'
How many late today?
There's mud all up the front staircase,
What is she going to say?

It's hot in here, I'm going to sneeze.
'All creatures great and small . . .'
A spider's dangling over her!
Where is it going to fall?

It might land softly in her hair –
would she feel it, d'you suppose?
Or, if it swung a little bit,
it might settle on her nose.

'All things wise and wonderful . . .'
The teachers stand in line.
It's only got an inch to go!
This may be a sign.

Oh, land on her, please land on her!
'The Lord God made them all . . .'
Then she'll forget she saw me there –
I was here, in Hall,

I wasn't late, I didn't leave
my footsteps on the stairs . . .
Oh! Spider, you must hurry up,
she's halfway through the prayers.

Spider, spider, burning bright . . .
'Three girls I want to see.
Where are you? You, and you, and . . . Oh!
What's this? Oh dear! Dear me! . . .'

A hundred eyes, eight hairy legs,
A shadow on the wall.
I wasn't there, I wasn't late.
The Lord God loves us all!

Jane Whittle

Morning Prayers

Late September, conker time,
Back at school the children file
Into the assembly hall.
Smells of freshly polished floors,
Disinfectants, sunlight soap,
Familiar sounds and smells will long
Recall those early days of school.
The day begins with morning prayers.

Headmaster strides into the hall,
Crowlike in black flapping gown,
And as the clock is striking nine,
He calls out, 'Silence please.'
And prayers begin.
The youngsters, like automatons
Repeat the words in all the same
Uncomprehending monotones,
'Ah Father wishart in Heaven,
Harold be thy name. . . .'

E. Graham Yooll

I Went Back

I went back after a cold
And nothing was the same.
When the register was called
Even my name
Sounded queer . . . new . . .
(And I was born here too!)
Everyone knew more than me,
Even Kenneth Hannaky
Who's worst usually.
They'd made a play
And puppets from clay
While I was away,
Learnt a song about Cape Horn,
Five guinea pigs were born.
Daffodils in the blue pot,
(I planted them)
Bloomed, and I was not
There to see.
Jean had a new coat
And someone, probably George,
Smashed my paper boat.
Monday was a dreadful day.
I wished I was still away.
Tuesday's news day.
I took my stamps to show,
Made a clown called Jo,
Learnt that song from John . . .
Cold's almost gone . . .
And . . . the smallest guinea pig,
Silky black and brown thing,
I'm having
Till spring.

Gwen Dunn

From the Classroom Window

Sometimes, when heads are deep in books,
And nothing stirs,
The sunlight touches that far hill,
And its three dark firs;
Then on those trees I fix my eyes –
And teacher hers.

Together awhile we contemplate
The air-blue sky
And those dark tree-tops; till, with a tiny
Start and sigh,
She turns again to the printed page –
And so do I.

But our two thoughts have met out there
Where no school is –
Where, among call of birds and faint
Shimmer of bees,
They rise in sunlight, resinous, warm –
Those dark fir-trees.

John Walsh

From the classroom window.

From the classroom window.
I can see trees looking like bands of
black lace.
The fringe of grass protecting the
frightened fence like tall thin body
guards.
The small sparrows black birds and
magpies looking like little midget
witches swooping down on their broom
sticks to get some food.

Neil Bartlett (aged 8)

Timothy Winters

Timothy Winters comes to school
With eyes as wide as a football—pool,
Ears like bombs and teeth like splinters:
A blitz of a boy is Timothy Winters.

His belly is white, his neck is dark,
And his hair is an exclamation-mark.
His clothes are enough to scare a crow
And through his britches the blue winds blow.

When teacher talks he won't hear a word
And he shoots down dead the arithmetic-bird,
He licks the patterns off his plate
And he's not even heard of the Welfare State.

Timothy Winters has bloody feet
And he lives in a house on Suez Street,
He sleeps in a sack on the kitchen floor
And they say there aren't boys like him any more.

Old Man Winters likes his beer
And his missus ran off with a bombardier,
Grandma sits in the grate with a gin
And Timothy's dosed with an aspirin.

The Welfare Worker lies awake
But the law's as tricky as a ten-foot snake,
So Timothy Winters drinks his cup,
And slowly goes on growing up.

At Morning Prayers the Master helves
For children less fortunate than ourselves,
And the loudest response in the room is when
Timothy Winters roars 'Amen!'

So come one angel, come on ten:
Timothy Winters says 'Amen
Amen amen amen amen,'
Timothy Winters, Lord.
                    Amen.

Charles Causley

Against Idleness and Mischief

How doth the little busy bee
   Improve each shining hour,
And gather honey all the day
   From every opening flower!

How skilfully she builds her cell!
   How neat she spreads the wax!
And labours hard to store it well
   With the sweet food she makes.

In works of labour or of skill
   I would be busy too;
For Satan finds some mischief still
   For idle hands to do.

In books, or work, or healthful play,
   Let my first years be passed,
That I may give for every day
   Some good account at last.

Isaac Watts

God Made the Bees

God made the bees,
The bees make the honey,
We do all the dirty work,
The teachers make the money.

Sent in by Lisa Adlard

36

Build a bonfire
Build a bonfire
Put the teacher at the top
Put headmaster in the middle
And burn the blooming lot.

Sent in by
Josephine Powney (aged 12)

Pounds, shillings, pence,
Teacher has no sense,
She came to school
To act the fool,
Pounds, shillings, pence.

Sir is kind and sir is gentle,
Sir is strong and sir is mental.

Land of soapy water,
Teacher's having a bath,
Headmaster's looking through the keyhole,
Having a jolly good laugh.

Sent in by Jane Whitfield

I had a dream last night,
A dream that made me laugh,
I dreamt I was a piece of soap,
In our headmistress's bath!

Sent in by Jackie Watts (aged 10)

My Teacher

Mrs Bond is nice she shouts
and makes me jump
and when she says get
your sum books out I
nearly faint and when she
says put on your pumps I
think I run round the world
and I run across the playground
and when she says run I run and when
she says jump I jump

Kevin Brown (aged 6)

Rodge Said

Rodge said,
'Teachers – they want it all ways –
You're jumping up and down on a chair
or something
and they grab hold of you and say
"Would you do that sort of thing in your own
home?"

'So you say, "No."
And they say,
"Well don't do it here then,"

'But if you say, "Yes, I do it at home."
they say,
"Well, we don't want that sort of thing
going on here
thank you very much."

'Teachers – they get you all ways,'
Rodge said.

Michael Rosen

Teacher's Pet

In the class there is usually a teacher's pet
Who is so goody goody.
Every class has one, no fret.
The girls are extra special teachers' pets (creeps!)
Teachers' pets do anything for the teachers –
'Yes, miss! No, miss! O.K. miss.
Anything you say, miss.'

Philip Moody (aged 9)

The Description of a Good Boy

The boy that is good,
Does learn his book well;
And if he can't read,
Will strive for to spell.

His school he does love,
And when he is there,
For play and for toys,
No time can he spare.

His mind is full bent,
On what he is taught;
He sits in the school,
As one full of thought.

Though not as a mope,
Who quakes out of fear
The whip or the rod
Should fall on his rear.

40

But like a good lad
Who aims to be wise,
He thinks on his book,
And not on his toys.

His mien will be grave,
Yet, if you would know,
He plays with an air,
When a dunce dare not so.

His aim is to learn,
His task is his play;
And when he has learned,
He smiles and looks gay.

Henry Dixon

There was an old man who said, 'Do
Tell me *how* I should add two and two?
    I think more and more
    That it makes about four –
But I fear that is almost too few.'

Anon

Maths Problems

Please add these up:
One ton of sawdust.
One ton of old newspaper.
Four tons of string.
One half-ton of fat.
Have you got all that in your head?
'Yes.'
I thought so.

Take any number.
Add ten.
Subtract three.
Now close your eyes.
(Your friend closes his eyes.)
Dark, isn't it!

Alvin Schwartz

Maths Lesson Rules

Always subtract bottom from top.
A plus and a plus equals a minus
or, a plus depending on the month
equals circumference but
equals fruit and pastry depending on the lesson.
Don't blow bubbles.
Remember to write who you love on desks
Don't eat the chalk
Come to lessons.
Don't sit on chairs – sit on the floor (it's safer).
Enter cupboards at your own risk.
Try to avoid flirting with new maths books.
Skive when possible. Don't get caught.
Look interested – in what's going on outside.
Cheat in exams.
Don't scribble rude words on the board
write them clearly.
Never go to detentions, or other dishonourable
                                        functions.
Don't pluck your eyebrows – save that for
                                        geography.

Christine Bates and Jill Etheridge

Exercise Book

Two and two four
four and four eight
eight and eight sixteen . . .
Once again! says the master
Two and two four
four and four eight
eight and eight sixteen.
But look! the lyre-bird
high on the wing
the child sees it
the child hears it
the child calls it.
Save me
play with me
bird!
So the bird alights
and plays with the child
Two and two four . . .
Once again! says the master
and the child plays
and the bird plays too . . .
Four and four eight
eight and eight sixteen
and twice sixteen makes what?
Twice sixteen makes nothing
least of all thirty-two
anyhow
and off they go.

For the child has hidden
the bird in his desk
and all the children
hear its song
and all the children
hear the music
and eight and eight in their turn
off they go
and four and four and two and two
in their turn fade away
and one and one make neither one nor two
but one by one off they go.
And the lyre–bird sings
and the child sings
and the master shouts
When you've quite finished playing the fool!
But all the children
are listening to the music
and the walls of the classroom
quietly crumble.
The windowpanes turn
once more to sand
the ink is sea
the desk is trees
the chalk is cliffs
and the quill pen
a bird again.

Jaques Prévert (translated by Paul Dehn)

Tingle-tangle Titmouse

Come hither, little piggy-wig,
Come and learn your letters,
And you shall have a knife and fork
To eat with, like your betters.
'Oh no,' the little pig replied,
'My trough will do as well;
I'd rather eat my victuals there
Than learn to read and spell.'

> With a tingle-tangle titmouse,
> Robin knows great A,
> B and C and D and E,
> F,G,H,I,J,K.

Come hither, little pussy-cat;
If you will grammar study,
I'll give you silver clogs to wear
Whene'er the weather's muddy.
'Oh, if I grammar learn,' said Puss,
'Your house will in a trice
Be overrun from top to bottom
With the rats and mice.'

> *Chorus*

Come hither, little puppy-dog;
I'll give you a new collar
If you will learn to read and spell
And be a clever scholar.
'Oh no,' the little dog replied,
'I've other fish to fry,
For I must learn to guard the house
And bark when thieves are nigh.'

> *Chorus*

Come hither then, good little boy,
And learn your alphabet,
And you a pair of boots and spurs
Like your papa shall get.
'Oh yes, I'll learn my alphabet;
And when I well can read,
My kind papa has promised me
A little long-tailed steed.'

With a tingle–tangle titmouse,
Robin knows great A,
B and C and D and E,
F,G,H,I,J,K.

Traditional

The ABC

'Twas midnight in the schoolroom
And every desk was shut,
When suddenly from the alphabet
Was heard a loud 'Tut-tut!'

Said A to B, 'I don't like C;
His manners are a lack.
For all I ever see of C
Is a semicircular back!'

'I disagree,' said D to B,
'I've never found C so.
From where *I* stand, he seems to be
An uncompleted O.'

C was vexed. 'I'm much perplexed,
You criticise my shape.
I'm made like that, to help spell Cat
And Cow and Cool and Cape.'

'He's right,' said E; said F, 'Whoopee!'
Said G, ''Ip, 'ip, 'ooray!'
'You're dropping me,' roared H to G.
'Don't do it please, I pray!'

'Out of my way,' LL said to K.
'I'll make poor I look Ill.'
To stop this stunt, J stood in front,
And presto! ILL was JILL.

'U know,' said V, 'that W
Is twice the age of me,
For as a Roman V is five
I'm half as young as he.'

X and Y yawned sleepily,
'Look at the time!' they said.
They all jumped in to beddy byes
And the last one in was Z!

Spike Milligan

Punctuation Puzzle

Caesar entered on his head
A helmet on each foot
A sandal in his hand he had
His trusty sword to boot.

BANANANANANANANANA

I thought I'd win the spelling bee
    And get right to the top,
But I started to spell 'banana,'
    And I didn't know when to stop.

William Cole

A was an Archer

A was an Archer, and shot at a frog,
B was a Blindman, and led by a dog.
C was a Cutpurse, and lived in disgrace,
D was a Drunkard, and had a red face.
E was an Eater, a glutton was he,
F was a Fighter, and fought with a flea.
G was a Giant, and pulled down a house,
H was a Hunter, and hunted a mouse.
I was an Ill man, and hated by all,
K was a Knave, and he robbed great and small.
L was a Liar, and told many lies,
M was a Madman, and beat out his eyes.
N was a Nobleman, nobly born,
O was an Ostler, and stole horses' corn.
P was a Pedlar, and sold many pins,
Q was a Quarreller, and broke both his shins.
R was a Rogue, and ran about town,
S was a Sailor, a man of renown.
T was a Tailor, and knavishly bent,
U was a Usurer, took ten per cent.
W was a Writer, and money he earned,
X was one Xenophon, prudent and learn'd.
Y was a Yeoman, and worked for his bread,
Z was one Zeno the Great, but he's dead.

Anon (1700)

A Good Poem

I like a good poem
one with lots of fighting
in it. Blood and the
clanging of armour. Poems

against Scotland are good
and poems that defeat
the French with crossbows.
I don't like poems that

aren't about anything.
Sonnets are wet and
a waste of time.
Also poems that don't

know how to rhyme.
If I was a poem
I'd play football and
get picked for England.

Roger McGough

Poets

We had two poets come to our school
today
I liked them.
They read poems
And one even tried to sing.
They told us about poetry.
We had two poets come to our school
today.
I liked them.

Elaine Breden

The English Language

Some words have different meanings,
and yet they're spelt the same.
A cricket is an insect,
to play it – it's a game.
On every hand, in every land,
it's thoroughly agreed,
the English language to explain,
is very hard indeed.

Some people say that you're a dear,
yet dear is far from cheap.
A jumper is a thing you wear,
yet a jumper has to leap.
It's very clear, it's very queer,
and pray who is to blame
for different meanings to some words
pronounced and spelt the same?

A little journey is a trip,
a trip is when you fall.
It doesn't mean you have to dance
whene'er you hold a ball.
Now here's a thing that puzzles me:
musicians of good taste
will very often form a band –
I've one around my waist!

You spin a top, go for a spin,
or spin a yarn may be –
yet every spin's a different spin,
as you can plainly see.
Now here's a most peculiar thing,
'twas told me as a joke –
a dumb man wouldn't speak a word,
yet seized a wheel and spoke.

A door may often be ajar,
but give the door a slam,
and then your nerves receive a jar –
and then there's jars of jam.
You've heard, of course, of traffic jams,
and jams you give your thumbs.
And adders, too, one is a snake,
the other adds up sums.

A policeman is a copper,
it's a nickname (impolite!)
yet a copper in the kitchen
is an article you light.
On every hand, in every land,
it's thoroughly agreed –
the English language to explain
is very hard indeed!

Harry Hemsley

Latin is a language
As dead as dead can be,
First it killed the Romans
And now it's killing me.

The English Succession

The Norman Conquest all historians fix
To the year of Christ, one thousand sixty-six.
Two Wills, one Henry, Stephen, Kings are
                                 reckoned;
Then rose Plantagenet in Henry second.
First Richard, John, third Henry, Edwards three,
And second Richard in one line we see.
Fourth, fifth, and sixth Lancastrian Henrys reign;
Then Yorkist Edwards two, and Richard slain.
Next Tudor comes in seventh Henry's right,
Who the red rose engrafted on the white.
Eighth Henry, Edward sixth, first Mary, Bess;
Then Scottish Stuart's right the peers confess.
James, double Charles, a second James expelled;
With Mary, Will; then Anne the sceptre held.
Last, Brunswick's issue has two Georges given;
Late may the second pass from earth to heaven!

Anon (c. 1749)

Willy, Willy

Willy, Willy, Harry, Stee
Harry, Dick, John, Harry Three
One, Two, Three Neds, Richard Two
Henry Four, Five, Six, then who?
Neds Four, Five and Dick the Bad,
Harrys Twain and Ned the Lad.
Mary, Bessie, James the Vain
Charley, Charley, James again.
William and Mary, Anna Gloria
Four Georges, William, and Victoria.
Edward Seventh, and then –
George the Fifth in 1910!

Demeanour

Busy in study be thou, child,
And in the hall, meek and mild,
And at the table, merry and glad,
And at bed, soft and sad.

Anon (c. 1525)

The Dunce

Why does he still keep ticking?
  Why does his round white face
Stare at me over the books and ink,
  And mock at my disgrace?
Why does that thrush call, 'Dunce, dunce, dunce!'?
  Why does that bluebottle buzz?
Why does the sun so silent shine? –
  And what do I care if it does?

Walter de la Mare

Streemin

Im in the botom streme
Which meens Im not brigth
dont like reading
cant hardly write

but all these divishns
arnt reely fair
look at the cemtery
no streemin there

Roger McGough

Confusion

Jean get licks in school today
For hitting Janet Hill
It was just after recess time
And class was playful still
Janet pull Jean ribbon off
And throw it on the ground
Jean got vex and cuff Janet
Same time Miss turn around
Miss didn't ask no questions
She just start beating Jean
Tomorrow Jean mother coming
to fix–up Miss McLean

Odette Thomas

The Bully Asleep

This afternoon, when grassy
Scents through the classroom crept,
Bill Craddock laid his head
Down on his desk, and slept.

The children came round him:
Jimmy, Roger, and Jane;
They lifted his head timidly
And let it sink again.

'Look, he's gone sound asleep, Miss,'
Said Jimmy Adair;
'He stays up all night, you see;
His mother doesn't care.'

'Stand away from him children.'
Miss Andrews stooped to see.
'Yes, he's asleep; go on
With your writing, and let him be.'

'Now's a good chance!' whispered Jimmy,
And he snatched Bill's pen and hid it.
'Kick him under the desk, hard;
He won't know who did it.'

'Fill all his pockets with rubbish –
Paper, apple-cores, chalk.'
So they plotted, while Jane
Sat wide-eyed at their talk.

Not caring, not hearing,
Bill Craddock he slept on;
Lips parted, eyes closed –
Their cruelty gone.

'Stick him with pins!' muttered Roger.
'Ink down his neck!' said Jim.
But Jane, tearful and foolish,
Wanted to comfort him.

John Walsh

Nooligan

I'm a nooligan
don't give a toss
in our class
I'm the boss
(well, one of them)

I'm a nooligan
got a nard 'ead
step out of line
and youre dead
(well, bleedin)

I'm a nooligan
I spray me name
all over town
footballs me game
(well, watchin)

I'm a nooligan
violence is fun
gonna be a nassassin
or a nired gun
(well, a soldier)

Roger McGough

Upon Pagget

Pagget, a school-boy, got a sword, and then
He vowed destruction both to birch, and men:
Who would not think this yonker fierce to fight?
Yet coming home, but somewhat late, (last night)
'Untruss,' his master bade him; and that word
Made him take up his shirt, lay down his sword.

Robert Herrick

Deborah Delora

Deborah Delora, she liked a bit of fun –
She went to the baker's and bought a penny bun;
Dipped the bun in treacle and threw it at her teacher –
Deborah Delora! What a wicked creature!

The Toe Picker

She is tall and likes to show off
She picks her toe nails
That's why I can't stand her
She takes off her smelly socks and picks at her toes
She doesn't care what anyone says
She is the worst show off at school
She is slim and moves lightly
But still she picks her toes
Skin all gone
Nail all gone
It looks disgusting
Everyone tells her to stop it
But she still picks her toes
She is pretty and has a lot of friends
Just because I am her sister
She picks her toes in front of me
But she still picks her toes
HORRID, NASTY, HORRID.

Debbie Ward

The Marrog

My desk's at the back of the class
    And nobody, nobody knows
        I'm a Marrog from Mars
With a body of brass
        And seventeen fingers and toes.

Wouldn't they shriek if they knew
    I've three eyes at the back of my head
And my hair is bright purple
My nose is deep blue
    And my teeth are half-yellow, half-red

My five arms are silver, and spiked
    With knives on them sharper than spears.
I could go back right now, if I liked –
    And return in a million light-years.

I could gobble them all,
For I'm seven foot tall
And I'm breathing green flames from my ears.

Wouldn't they yell if they knew,
    If they guessed that a Marrog was here?
Ha-ha, they haven't a clue –
    Or wouldn't they tremble with fear!
'Look, look, a Marrog'
    They'd all scream – and SMACK
The blackboard would fall and the ceiling would
                                        crack
    And teacher would faint, I suppose.
But I grin to myself, sitting right at the back
    And nobody, nobody knows.

                                        R. C. Scriven

Scribbled on the Fly-leaves in Old School Books

Black is the raven
Black is the rook
But blacker the sinner
Who pinches this book.

This book is mine
This boot another
Touch not the one
For fear of the other.

He what takes what isn't his'n
When he's cotched, will go to prison.

Good News

The Board of Education has just set up new rules
That in the future they'll shut all the schools
On every April Fool's.

APRIL FOOL!
(Keep cool.)

William Cole

Board Rubber

Board rubber you're dusty
I bet you learn a lot
That concludes today's lesson.

Gina Staley

Last Lesson of the Day

Here we come,
Only to be trapped in,
For the agonising,
Moments of the day.
Through the door,
Down with the bag,
And up with the desk,
'Get that desk down,'
''Ere we go again.'
'Get out your work – quietly.'
The last moments lingered on,
Like a weary dog
Being pulled along by an impatient master.
Come on, the bell must ring,
Drrrrrrrinnnnggggggggggg!
Up with the desk,
In with the books,
Up with the bag
And out the door all as fast as
GREASE LIGHTENING.

Chris Palmer

SONGS

Mary had a little lamb,
  Its feet were black as soot,
And into Mary's bread and jam
  Its sooty foot it put.

Mary had a little lamb,
  It was a greedy glutton.
She fed it on ice-cream all day
  And now it's frozen mutton.

Mary had a little lamb,
  She ate it with mint sauce,
And everywhere that Mary went
  The lamb went too, of course.

Mary had a wristlet watch,
  She swallowed it one day,
And now she's taking Beecham's pills
  To pass the time away.

Mary had a little *cow*,
  It fed on safety pins;
And every time she milked the cow
  The milk came out in tins.

Never let your braces dangle,
Never let your braces dangle.
Poor old sport
He got caught
And went right through the mangle;
Went through the mangle he did, by gum,
Came out like linoleum,
Now he sings in kingdom-come:
Never let your braces dangle, chum.

I'm a knock-kneed chicken, I'm a bow-legged
                               sparrow,
Missed my bus so I went by barrow.
I went to the café for my dinner and my tea,
Too many radishes – Hick! Pardon me.

I went to the animal fair,
All the birds and the beasts were there,
The gay baboon by the light of the moon
Was combing his yellow hair.
The monkey fell from his bunk
And dropped on the elephant's trunk.
The elephant sneezed, and went down on his knees
And what became of the mon-key,
      mon-key, mon-key, mon-key,
      monk?

There was a bloomin' spider,
Climbed up a bloomin' spout,
Down came the rain
And washed the spider out.
Out came the sunshine
Dried up all the rain,
Up the bloomin' water spout
The blighter went again.

There's a long, long worm a-crawling
Across the roof of my tent.
I can hear the whistle calling,
And it's time I went.
There's the cold, cold water waiting
For me to take my morning dip.
And when I come back I'll find that worm
Upon my pillow-slip.

The Yellow Rose of Texas and the man from
                                        Laramie
Went down to Davy Crockett's to have a cup of tea;
The tea was so delicious, they had another cup,
And poor old Davy Crockett had to do the
                                        washing up.

After the ball was over
She lay on the sofa and sighed.
She put her false teeth in salt water
And took out her lovely glass eye.
She kicked her cork leg in the corner
And hung up her wig on the wall,
The rest of her went to bye-byes,
After the ball.

Mademoiselle from Armentières, parlez-vous,
She hasn't been kissed for forty years, parlez-vous.
The Prince of Wales was put in jail
For riding a horse without a tail,
Inky-pinky parlez-vous.

        Jingle bells,
        Batman smells,
        Robin flew away,
        Kojak lost his lollipop
        And found it straight away.

Sent in by Jonathan David Riddell (aged 7)

Carols

'*We Three Kings* of Orient are
Trying to light a rubber cigar.'
It was loaded and exploded
Blowing them all afar.

We four Beatles of Liverpool are,
John in a taxi, Paul in a car,
George on a scooter, tooting his hooter,
Following Ringo Starr.

While Shepherds washed their socks by night
All seated round the tub,
A bar of Sunlight soap came down
And they began to scrub.

While shepherds watched their turnip tops
All boiling in the pot,
A lump of soot came rolling down
And spoilt the bloomin' lot.

Good King Wenceslas looked out
　　On the Feast of Stephen;
A snowball hit him on the snout
　　And made it all uneven.
Brightly shone his conk that night
　　Though the pain was cruel,
Till the doctor came in sight
　　Riding on a mu–oo–el.

Good King Wenceslas walked out
　　In his mother's garden.
He bumped into a Brussels sprout
　　And said 'I beg your pardon'.

Good King Wenceslas looked out
　　When he was on 'telly',
Chased his page all round the screen
　　And punched him in the belly.

Hark! the jelly babies sing,
Beecham's pills are just the thing,
They are gentle, meek and mild,
Two for a man and one for a child.
If you want to go to heaven
You must take a dose of seven;
If you want to go to hell,
Take the blinking box as well.

Nicky-nacky-noo

With my hands on my head, what have I here?
This is my brain-box, and nothing to fear.
Brain-box and nicky-nacky-noo,
That's what they taught me when I went to school.

With my hands on my eyes, what have I here?
These are my eye-blinkers, nothing to fear.
Eye-blinkers, brain-box, and nicky-nacky-noo,
That's what they taught me when I went to school.

With my hands on my nose, what have I here?
This is my nose-wiper, nothing to fear.
Nose-wiper, eye-blinkers,
Brain-box and nicky-nacky-noo,
That's what they taught me when I went to school.

With my hands on my mouth, what have I here?
This is my mouth-clicker, nothing to fear.
Mouth-clicker, nose-wiper, eye-blinkers,
Brain-box and nicky-nacky-noo,
That's what they taught me when I went to school.

With my hands on my chin, what have I here?
This is my chin-chopper, nothing to fear.
Chin-chopper, mouth-clicker,
Nose-wiper, eye-blinkers,
Brain-box and nicky-nacky-noo,
That's what they taught me when I went to school.

With my hands on my chest, what have I here?
This is my chest-protector, nothing to fear.
Chest-protector, chin-chopper,
Mouth-clicker, nose-wiper, eye-blinkers,
Brain-box and nicky-nacky-noo,
That's what they taught me when I went to school.

With my hands on my tum, what have I here?
This is my bread-box, and nothing to fear.
Bread-box, chest-protector,
Chin-chopper, mouth-clicker,
Nose-wiper, eye-blinkers,
Brain-box and nicky-nacky-noo,
That's what they taught me when I went to school.

With my hands on my knees, what have I here?
These are my knee-benders, nothing to fear.
Knee-benders, bread-box,
Chest-protector, chin-chopper,
Mouth-clicker, nose-wiper, eye-blinkers,
Brain-box and nicky-nacky-noo,
That's what they taught me when I went to school.

Traditional

Songs

(remembered by poet Seamus Heaney, as chanted on the way to and from school, in County Derry, Ireland, in the '40s).

One fine October's morning September last July
The moon lay thick upon the ground, the mud
                              shone in the sky.
I stepped into a tramcar to take me across the sea,
I asked the conductor to punch my ticket, he
                              punched my eye for me.

I fell in love with an Irish girl, she sang me an Irish
                              dance,
She lived in Tipperary, just a few miles out of
                              France.
The house it was a round one, the front was at the
                              back,
It stood alone between two more, and it was
                              whitewashed black.

Speech Day

Ladles and Jellyspoons,
I stand upon this speech to make a platform,
The train I arrived in has not yet come,
So I took a bus and walked.
I come before you
To stand behind you
And tell you something
I know nothing about.

Wycombe Abbey Song

When the holidays are over, and the term is well
                                              begun,
When our lesson books are put away, and the
                                    morning's work is done,
Then we rush forth from the boot room, before the
                                       clock strikes two,
For all of us are very keen to play lacrosse anew.

> *Chorus*
> Pass, catch, pass again. Keep it in the air.
> Now the centre's caught it, so down the field
>   we tear.

Now the hockey season follows and our sticks are
                                          routed out,
When we've bullied at the centre, we begin to slash
                                              about.
We're fighting for our honour, for we want to win
                                          the cup,
And the lusty shouts around us bid us not to give it
                                              up.

76

Chorus
HIC, HAC, HOC away, set it on the roll.
Pass it down to somebody and quickly shoot a
goal.

But the summer term is best for we are out from
morn to night,
Then we run out to play cricket as soon as it is light.
And we lie beneath the beeches when the sun is
overhead,
Then cricket in the evening till it's time to go to bed.

Chorus
Slog, run, run again, you're running up the
score.
Now do look out for catches. How's that for
leg before?

Written in 1902

School Song of Godolphin and Latimer School, Hammersmith

Rising early in the morning we proceed to Iffley
                                              Road
Every girl herself adorning with a scarlet duffle
                                              hood.
  Each is fearful lest too late
  She should come inside the gate.
  By the Staff-room we foregather
  Or perchance to read the weather
(Take a friend along for luck in either case).
When the dinner-money's checked
  All the home-work we collect,
Alphabetically, every book in place.
So very soon our lessons have begun,
We hope we shan't forget them everyone.
First of all we try to wrestle with some French,
And then we have to give our minds a wrench
To penetrate the mystery of Elizabethan history;
It's a rather tiresome business, we forget the names
                                              and dates.

  Then the break bell makes us hurry,
  All is bustle, haste and scurry
To the table where we drink our milk provided by
                                            · the State.

  Thus refreshed we go to battle
  With hard problems about cattle.
'If six cows could eat a bale of hay, how much could
                                              sixty eat?'
  Spend a little time in singing
  Or perhaps some minutes clinging
To the ropes in the gymnasium, with the aid of
                                              hands and feet.

There's a long, long queue for dinner
    (Every moment we feel thinner)
But we have a little gossip on the way.
    Then we eat our lunch and chatter,
    (Every moment growing fatter)
Though there's never time for all we have to say.
But the bell rings loud and long at just 2.10.
And hard at work each girl may soon be then.
Some learn how they should choose a piece of meat
And how to cook and make it fit to eat.
    Others brush and pencil bearing
    To the Art Room swift repairing
Draw and paint familiar figures (they can do it
                              rather well).

    Some spend afternoons at science
    Learn to use each weird appliance
And on the air comes floating many a strange and
                            wondrous smell.

    After school it is a pleasure
    To play hockey in full measure
Watch a match or practise singing, tune our fiddles,
                           join debate.

    Then in shine, or shower or rain,
    For the trolley bus or train
With our harrowing thoughts of homework we
                    go hurrying through the gate.
    Chorus So we hail the 4th of May
              When we keep the school's birthday
              With dance and song and music and
                    with celebrations meet.
              It's a privilege and pleasure
              Which we treasure beyond measure
For the Dolphin school's delightful and it's very
                    hard to beat.

Pontefract and District High School School Song

It isn't only lessons
We come to school to learn,
E'en here we know the changes
Of Fortune, kind or stern.
We cannot all gain prizes
We can't win every game,
But though we're disappointed,
We love School just the same.

But one day we must leave it
And 'mid the world's stern strife
We'll know another teacher,
The great Headmistress Life.
Then may our old School's honour
Be still our proudest boast,
And may we e'er prove worthy
Of Her who taught us most.

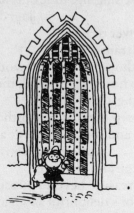

SCHOOL DINNERS

TODAYS
MENU
COOKS
FLUFFY
DUMPLINGS

A Child's Grace

Here a little child I stand
Heaving up my either hand;
Cold as paddocks though they be,
Here I lift them up to Thee,
For a benison to fall
On our meat and on us all. Amen.

Robert Herrick

Dinner Lady

'Hold your plate a little nearer, dear,
if you want any gravy. – Someone's 'ere
changing the electric, all the plugs,
I couldn't boil the water up – those mugs
are there to put yer tea in, Jean. –
Hey! Mighty Mouse, where've you been
to get in such an awful dirty mess?
Go back and wash your face again! Who'd guess
you'd got a mother and a house an' home?
I've never ever seen you use a comb.
– As I was saying, couldn't even heat it. –
What d'you think we're here for? You must eat it!
– I says to 'im, not Mr H, – ter Bob,
"You gotta fix it now, it's your job
to keep things working 'ere; and we'll do ours
if you do yours, O.K.?" What dinner hours
do we get, me or you? When I'm through
I can't put me feet up, no more can you,

as like as not the rotten bus is late . . . –
Watch it, lad! Hold still, let's 'ave your plate.
– or all the shops 'ave shut before we're free
and then it's time to cook again for tea
and feed our own at 'ome, to fill his belly,
wash it up again while they watch telly
and still a pile of ironing to be done . . . –
Give it 'ere, that's cabbage, my ol' son.
No! Shepherd's pie, my pet, not sheep!
You funny child! – They make you weep.
God knows the kind of things they eat at 'ome,
no wonder some are only skin and bone,
with biscuits, crisps and pop an' sweets an' all
I don't think some mums cook their food at all. –
Don't push like that up there, stand still!
We'll not be serving seconds, not until
you let those other girls come through, and then
just to those as can behave . . . and when
you can stop that yelling at the back.
– Roll on Sunday, I say! – Shirley Black,
get that hair of yours from off the cheese!
Warren, use your hanky when you sneeze!
– Do their parents teach them anything?
You often wonder. – Sharon, will you bring
those dirty plates up when you queue for sweet?
– D'you know, half the kids that live in our street
don't get in till after ten at night?
Small wonder they look a pathetic sight
in morning school. But still, one thing that's good,
they get their midday dinners free. Hot food
is just what this lot need. – Let's 'ave that spoon.
– They do look better in the afternoon!'

Jane Whittle

83

Dinner Lady

I kissed the dinner lady
In a strange romantic dream.
Her cheeks blushed prettily
As strawberries with cream.

I kissed the dinner lady
And in my sleep I sighed.
I stroked her hair, as sooty black
As mushroom's underside.

I kissed the dinner lady,
My eyes closed quietly.
Like cool and fresh green watercress
Her clear eyes looked at me.

I kissed the dinner lady
As I lay drowsily,
She smiled at me with teeth as white
As crisp blanched celery.

I kissed the dinner lady
In a sleepy reverie.
Her lips were cool as lettuce leaves
As she pressed them on to me.

Now I kiss the dinner lady
Every meal-time of my life.
She is my cordon bleu girl
She is my loving wife.

Robert Sparrow

School Dinners

You go to school dinners,
You sit side by side,
You cannot escape –
Many have tried.
You look at the gravy,
All lumpy and still,
If that doesn't get you
The custard will.

Sent in by Philip Moody (aged 9)

School dinners, school dinners,
Burnt baked beans, burnt baked beans,
Sloppy semolina, sloppy semolina,
I feel sick,
Get a bucket quick.

The sausage is a cunning bird
With feathers long and wavy;
It swims about the frying pan
And makes its nest in gravy.

There was a young lad of St Just
Who ate apple pie till he bust;
    It wasn't the fru-it
    That caused him to do it,
What finished him off was the crust.

Cherry Stones

*This is the rhyme you recite when counting
the cherry stones left on your plate.*

Who will I marry?
Tinker Tailor Soldier Sailor Rich Man
Poor Man Beggarman Thief
What will his name be?
A B C D . . .
What will I drive to Church in?
Coach Carriage Wheelbarrow Donkeycart.
What will I wear?
Silk Satin Cotton Rags.
Boots Shoes Sandals Clogs.
What will I live in?
Big House Little House Pigsty Barn.
How many children will I have?
1 2 3 4 . . .

Blotting Paper Pudding

Blotting paper pudding's a dish fit for a queen,
The mixture of ingredients, it really must be seen;
There's best black ink and gunpowder, and sealing
                                                wax as well,
And smudgy chalk, pink white and blue – the
                                          method now I'll tell.

For blotting paper pudding's a dish fit for a queen,
The way you set about it, it really must be seen.
You tear it up, and mix it up, and slosh it all about,
You give a stir, and take a sup, and then let out a
                                                shout –

Oh! blotting paper pudding's a dish fit for a queen,
A stranger dish you'll never find, it really must be
                                                seen
The cooking is the tricky bit, it's really quite an art,
The time and heat must be just right, before you
                                          make a start,

Then blotting paper pudding's a dish fit for a queen,
The recipe is quite unique, it really must be seen.
The taste is so astonishing, I'm sure you will agree,
It's sour, and sharp, and powdery, and bitter as can
be.

But blotting paper pudding's a dish fit for a queen,
My best invention ever, it really must be seen,
And when the work has all been done, and you can
feast your eyes,
I know you'll say, 'Well done, White Knight –
you've won the pudding prize!'

Jenny Craig

Humpty Dumpty sat on the wall
Eating black bananas.
Where d'you think he put the skins?
Down the king's pyjamas.

Sent in by Lucy Floyer (aged 4)

Poor Simon Benn

Poor Simon Benn
Poor Simon Benn
His sandwiches are frozen again,

All night long left in deep-freeze.
Now surely Mum intended to please
And not to vex, torment or tease.

It's no fun lunching
Cheek muscles bunching
Ice crystals crunching.

Mrs Benn please
Not steel-hard cheese
At zero degrees.

Please, Mrs Benn
Please, Mrs Benn
His sandwiches are frozen again.

Robert Sparrow

Mary ate jam,
Mary ate jelly,
Mary went home
With a pain in her –
Now don't get excited
Don't be misled
Mary went home
With a pain in her head.

Table Rules for Little Folk

In silence I must take my seat,
And give God thanks before I eat;
Must for my food in patience wait,
Till I am asked to hand my plate;
I must not scold, nor whine, nor pout,
Nor move my chair nor plate about;
With knife, or fork, or napkin ring,
I must not play, nor must I sing.
I must not speak a useless word,
For children should be seen, not heard;
I must not talk about my food,
Nor fret if I don't think it good;
I must not say, 'The bread is old,'
'The tea is hot,' 'The coffee's cold';
My mouth with food I must not crowd,
Nor while I'm eating speak aloud;
Must turn my head to cough or sneeze,
And when I ask, say 'If you please';
The tablecloth I must not spoil,
Nor with my food my fingers soil;
Must keep my seat whan I have done,
Nor round the table sport or run;
When told to rise, then I must put
My chair away with noiseless foot;
And lift my heart to God above,
In praise for all his wondrous love.

Anon (c. 1858)

Table Manners

The Goops they lick their fingers,
    And the Goops they lick their knives;
They spill their broth on the table-cloth;
    Oh, they live untidy lives.
The Goops they talk while eating,
    And loud and fast they chew,
So that is why I am glad that I
    Am not a Goop. Are you?

Gelett Burgess

Scottish Grace

Some hae meat that canna eat
    And some could eat that want it;
But we hae meat and we can eat,
    For which the Lord be thankit!

Anon

PLAYTIME

OUR HEADMASTER MISTER GUMM
HAS GOT A PIMPLE ON

The Battle

Our janitor was tortured in the war,
The Boer War, I suppose,
So Pete reckoned we should have a battle
Down by the janny's hut.
It was fitting, I suppose.

I was Winston Churchill,
Bill was General Custer,
Joe was Julius Caesar
And Pete was Alfred the Great.
The one who burnt the cakes, I suppose.

Our janny was Adolf Hitler.
Our janny was Attila the Hun,
Our janny was Sitting Bull
And Wilfred, the school dog, was
His horse, I suppose.

In the dead of night
We circled our janitor's hut.
Joe had nicked some matches from his dad
And we flicked them through the dark,
Instead of bullets, I suppose.

Our janny's hut caught fire
And burned to the ground as we fled.
The night's silence returned,
Interrupted only by a far-off howling.
Wilfred, the school dog, I suppose.

Benjamin Bolt

Children's Song

Johnnie Crack and Flossie Snail
Kept their baby in a milking pail
Flossie Snail and Johnnie Crack
One would pull it out and one would put it back
O it's my turn now said Flossie Snail
To take the baby from the milking pail
And it's my turn now said Johnnie Crack
To smack it on the head and put it back

Johnnie Crack and Flossie Snail
Kept their baby in a milking pail
One would put it back and one would pull it out
And all it had to drink was ale and stout
For Johnnie Crack and Flossie Snail
Always used to say that stout and ale
Was *good* for a baby in a milking pail

Dylan Thomas (from 'Under Milk Wood')

Dips – to Start a Game

Dip!
Ickery, ahry, oary, ah,
Biddy, barber, oary, sah,
Peer, peer, mizter, meer,
Pit, pat, out one.

Eeny, meeny, miney, mo,
Sit the baby on the po,
When he's done,
Wipe his bum,
Tell his mummy what he's done.

Oh deary me,
Mother caught a flea,
Put it in the kettle
To make a cup of tea.
The flea jumped out,
And bit mother's snout,
In came daddy
With his shirt hanging out.

Paddy on the railway
Picking up stones;
Along came an engine
And broke Paddy's bones.
Oh, said Paddy,
That's not fair.
Pooh, said the engine-driver,
I don't care.

Hickety pickety i sillickety
Pompalorum jig,
Every man who has no hair
Generally wears a wig.
One, two, three,
Out goes he.

Eenty, teenty, orry, ram, tam, toosh,
Ging in alow the bed, and catch a wee fat moose.
Cut it up in slices, and fry it in a pan,
Mind and keep the gravy for the wee fat man.

Ip, dip, dalabadi,
Dutch cheese, santami,
Santa mi, dalabadi,
Sham.

One-ery, oo–ry, ick–ry, an,
Bipsy, bopsy, little Sir Jan,
Queery, quaury,
Virgin Mary,
Nick, tick, toloman tick,
O–U–T, out,
Rotten, totten, dish–clout,
Out jumps – He.

Mickey Mouse bought a house,
What colour did he paint it?
Shut your eyes and think.
– RED.
R–E–D spells red,
And out you must go for saying so
With a clip across your ear–hole.

Hinty, minty, cuty, corn,
Apple seed, and apple thorn,
Wire, briar, limber lock,
Three geese in a flock.
One flew east, and one flew west,
One flew over the cuckoo's nest.
    Up on yonder hill.
That is where my father dwells;
He has jewels, he has rings,
He has many pretty things.
He has a hammer with two nails,
He has a cat with twenty tails.
Strike Jack, lick Tom!
    Blow the bellows, old man!

Clapping Games

Who stole the buns from the bakery shop?
Number one stole the buns from the bakery shop.
Who, me?
Yes, you!
Couldn't have been me,
Number two stole the buns from the bakery shop.
Who, me?
Yes, you!
Couldn't have been me,
Number three stole the buns from the bakery
shop. . .

Um pom pay carolay carolester
Um pom pay carolay
Ickidideely so far lee
Ickidideely pouf pouf.

I am Popeye the sailor man – full stop –
I live in a caravan – full stop –
And when I go swimming
I kiss all the women
I am Popeye the sailor man –
Full stop, full stop,
Comma, comma,
Dash, Dash.

I went to a Chinese restaurant to buy a loaf of bread,
He asked me what my surname was, and this is
what I sai–ai–aid,

'Zom pom poodle
Allawalie whisky
Chinese chopsticks
Indian squawful
O–o–o–o–o
How!'

Under the bamboo,
Under the sea,
Boom, boom, boom!
True love for me, my darling,
True love for you.
And when we're married
We'll raise a family,
And so it's under the bamboo,
Under the sea.

Tommy broke a bottle
And blamed it on me.
I told Ma
Ma told Pa
Tommy got a whacking
On his Oom pa pa!

100

I am a girl guide dressed in blue,
These are the actions I can do –
Salute to the captain,
Curtsey to the queen,
Show my panties to the football team.

I had the German measles
I had them really bad,
They wrapped me up in blankets
And threw me in the van,
The van was very shaky
I nearly fell out,
But when I got to hospital
I heard the children shout –
'Mummy, Daddy, take me home
I've been here a year or so.'
In came Dr Alastair
Sliding down the banister,
Half way down he split his pants
Now he's doing the ballet dance.

Jumping Game

Cat's got the measles,
Dog's got the flu,
Chicken's got the chicken pox,
And so have you.

*All sent in by girls from
Downton Primary School*

Child's Bouncing Song

Molly Vickers
wets her knickers,
Georgie's father's big and black,
cream on Sunday
milk on Monday,
I'm the cock of all the back.

Tell me who's a
bigger boozer
Mister Baker beats them all,
from his lorry
watch him hurry,
touch the ground and touch the wall.

Who're the gentry
down our entry – Mrs Smith's got two TV's.
What if her coat
is a fur coat,
all her kids are full of fleas.

Joan loves Harry,
Jack will marry
Edna when they both grow up,
I'll announce it,
bounce bounce bounce it,
our dog Whisker's had a pup.

High and low and
to and fro and
down the street and up the hill,
Mrs Cuthbert's
husband snuffed it,
she got nothing from his will.

Mister, mister,
Shirley's sister
won a prize on Blackpool prom,
mam'll smother
our kid brother
when the school inspectors come.

Skip and hopping
I'm off shopping,
Tuesday night it's pie for tea,
please to take this
ball and make this
song a bouncing song for me.

Tony Connor

Ball Bouncing

Bounce ball! Bounce ball!
One, two, three.
Underneath my right leg
And round about my knee.
Bounce ball! Bounce ball!
Bird-or-bee
Flying from the rose-bud
Up into the tree.

Bounce ball! Bounce ball!
Fast-you-go.
Underneath my left leg
And round about my toe.
Bounce ball! Bounce ball!
Butt-er-fly
Flying from the rose-bud
Up into the sky.

Long-legged Italy
Kicked poor Sicily
Into the middle of the Mediterranean Sea.
Austria was Hungary,
Took a bit of Turkey,
Dipped it in Greece,
Fried it in Japan,
And ate it off China.

Skipping Rhymes

A frog walked into a public house,
   and asked for a pint of beer.
'Where's your money?'
   'In my pocket.'
'Where's your pocket?'
   'I forgot it.'
'Well, please walk out.'

        Eaver Weaver, chimney sweeper,
           Had a wife and couldn't keep her,
        Had another, didn't love her,
           Up the chimney he did shove her.

Tiddly Wink the barber,
Went to shave his father,
    The razor slip
    and cut his lip,
Tiddly Wink the barber.

        Good King Wenceslas,
        Knocked a bobby senseless,
        Right in the middle of
        Marks and Spencers.

Julius Caesar,
The Roman Geezer,
Squashed his wife
With a lemon squeezer.

All sent in by Ceri Broomhead (aged 11)

105

One o'clock, two o'clock, three o'clock, four,
In comes (Polly) through the door.
Five o'clock, six o'clock, seven o'clock, eight,
Out goes (Polly) through the gate.

I like coffee, I like tea,
I like the boys and they like me.
So tell your ma to hold her tongue
'Cos she had a boy when she was young.
And tell your pa to do the same,
'Cos he was the one who changed her name.

Jelly on the plate, jelly on the plate
Wibble wobble wibble wobble
Jelly on the plate.
Custard on the spoon, custard on the spoon
Lick it off, lick it off
Custard on the spoon.
Sausage in the pan, sausage in the pan
One goes pop
And the other goes bang.

Redcurrant, blackcurrant, raspberry tart,
Tell me the name of your sweetheart:
A B C D . . .

One two, buckle my shoe
Three four, shut the door
Five six, pick up sticks
Seven eight, lay them straight
Nine ten, a big fat hen
Eleven twelve, dig and delve
Thirteen fourteen, maids a-courting
Fifteen sixteen, maids a-milking
Seventeen eighteen, maids a-baking
Nineteen twenty, my plate's empty:
Please give me some *tea!*

1 2 3 4 5 6 7,
All good children go to heaven.
Penny on the water
Tuppence on the sea
Threepence on the railway,
And *out goes she!*

One two three *O'Lary*
I spy sister *Mary*
Sitting on a *pompalary*
Eating chocolate *wafers.*

Salt Mustard Vinegar Pepper,
French Almond Rock.
Bread and butter for your supper
That's all mother's got.
Fish and chips and coca cola,
Pig's head and trout.
Bread and butter for your supper,
O.U.T. spells *out*.

Peter *Pan* bread and *jam*
Marmalade and *treacle*.
A bit for *you* and a bit for *me*
And *none* for naughty people.

I had a little *sausage*,
A little German *sausage*,
I put it in the pan for me *tea*.
I went out playing,
And I heard the sausage saying
Ellen, Ellen, Ellen, come in for your tea.

Charlie Chaplin washing up
Broke a basin and a cup.
How much did they cost?
10p – 20p – 30p – . . .

Teddy bear, teddy bear
Touch the ground.
Teddy bear, teddy bear
Turn around.
Teddy bear, teddy bear
Jump upstairs.
Teddy bear, teddy bear
Say your prayers.
Teddy bear, teddy bear
Blow out the light.
Teddy bear, teddy bear
Say goodnight!

Two, four, six, eight,
Mary at the cottage gate,
Eating cherries off a plate.
Two, four, six, eight.

All in together
This fine weather.
When it's your birthday,
Please run out.
    January, February, March . . .
All in together
This fine weather.
When it's your birthday
Please run in.
    1st, 2nd, 3rd . . .

Nebuchadnezzar the King of the Jews
Bought his wife a pair of shoes.
When the shoes began to wear
Nebuchadnezzar began to swear.

Over the garden wall
I let the baby fall.
My mother came out
And gave me a shout
Over the garden wall.

Over the garden wall
I let the baby fall.
My father came out
And gave me a clout
Over the garden wall.

Belfast Skipping Song

Datsie-dotsie, miss the rope, you're outie-o,
If you'd've been, where I'd have been,
You wouldn't have been put outie-o,
All the money's scarce, people out of workie-o,
Datsie-dotsie, miss the rope, you're outie-o.

Conkers

Conker Jeremy,
My first blow,
Conker Jack,
My first whack.

    Ally, ally, onker,
    My first conker,
    Quack, quack,
    My first smack.

Obbly, onker,
My first conker,
Obbly oh,
My first go.

Winter

On Winter mornings in the playground
The boys stand huddled,
Their cold hands doubled
Into trouser pockets.
The air hangs frozen
About the buildings
And the cold is an ache in the blood
And a pain on the tender skin
Beneath finger nails.
The odd shouts
Sound off like struck iron
And the sun
Balances white
Above the boundary wall.
I fumble my bus ticket
Between numb fingers
Into a fag,
Take a drag
And blow white smoke
Into the December air.

Gareth Owen

Words

Sticks and stones
May break my bones
But words can never hurt me –
That is what I'm supposed to say.
But:
'One, two, three,
Bri–an Lee –
His mother picks his fleas,
She roasts them,
She toasts them,
They have them for their teas.'

Sticks and stones
May break my bones
But words can never hurt me –
That is what I say.

But:
'One, two, three,
Bri–an Lee
Went to sea,
A big fish swam up
Got him by the knee.
The boat turned over,
Brian couldn't swim.
I wonder whatever
Happened to him.'

Sticks and stones
May break my bones
But. . . .
'One, two, three,
Bri–an Lee
Went for a pee –
Never came back.
Found him later,
Put him in a sack.'

Sticks and stones. . . .
But. . . .
Words can prick,
Can pierce, can sting,
Can cut, can stab,
Can scar, can sling.
This is what I shout back:

'George Rudden
Is fat as a pig,
He eats so much pudden
His belly gets big.'

'Mary McVicker's
Brain's gone numb,
When she bends over
We can all see her bum.
She's forgot to put them on –
No-knickers
Mary McVickers.'

'Freddy Bell
's got feet that smell –
He won't change his socks.
Shut him in a cell,
Drop him down a well,
Nail him in a box.'

But. . . .
They won't clear off.
Nothing I say
Seems quite good enough
To hurt them as much
As they hurt me. . . .
Though I stand and shout
Till some mister comes out
And tells me to go away.

Sticks and stones
May break my bones –

With a pound of plaster
Your bones get better –
But once it's been heard,
Who forgets the Word?

Brian Lee

The Fight

The kick off is
I don't like him;
Nothing about him.
He's fat and soft;
Like a jellybaby he is.
Now he's never done nothing,
Not to me,
He wouldn't dare:
Nothing at all of anything like that.
I just can't stand him,
So I'll fight him
And I'll beat him,
I could beat him any day.

The kick off is, it's his knees:
They knock together,
They sock together.
And they're fat,
With veins that run into his socks
Too high.
Like a girl he is,
And his shorts,
Too long,
They look
All wrong,
Like a Mum's boy.
Then
He simpers and dimples,
Like a big lass he is;
So I'll fight him
Everyone beats him,
I could beat him any day.

For another thing it's his hair,
All smarmed and oily fair,
All silk and parted flat,
His Mum does it like that
With her flat hand and water,
All licked and spittled into place,
With the quiff all down his face.
And his satchel's new
With his name in blue
Chalked on it.
So I chalked on it,
'Trevor is a cissie'
On it.
So he's going to fight me,
But I'll beat him,
I could beat him any day.

There's a crowd behind the sheds
When we come they turn their heads
Shouting and laughing,
Wanting blood and a bashing.
Take off my coat, rush him,
Smash him, bash him
Lash him, crash him
In the head,
In the bread
Basket.

Crack, thwack,
He's hit me back
Shout and scream
'Gerroff me back,
Gerroff, gerroff!
You wait, I'll get you,
I could beat you any day!'

Swing punch, bit his hand.
Blood on teeth, blood on sand.
Buttons tear, shouts and sighs,
Running nose, tears in eyes.

I'll get him yet; smack him yet.
Smash his smile, teacher's pet.
Brow grazed by knuckle
Knees begin to buckle.
'Gerroff me arms you're hurtin' me!'
'Give in?'
'No.'
'Give in?'
'No. Gerroff me arms!'
'Give in?'
'No.'
'Give in?'
'GIVE IN?'
'NEVER.'
'GIVE IN?'
'OOOH GERROFF GERROFF.'
'GIVE IN?'
'I . . . give . . . in . . . yeah.'

Don't cry, don't cry,
Wipe tears from your eye.
Walk home all alone
In the gutters all alone.
Next time I'll send him flying,
I wasn't really trying;
I could beat him any day.

Gareth Owen

The Bully

One of the girls at Audrey's school
Would terrify the others.
She'd talk about a Creep that lurks
And of a Thing that smothers.

She'd tell them that she'd be in touch
(Unless they gave her stuff
Like necklaces and sharpeners)
With the beasts that acted tough.

The children were too scared to tell
And never explained fully
About this girl, whom we won't name,
Except to call her bully.

Fay Maschler

Hill Rolling

I kind of exploded inside,
and joy shot out of me.
I began my roll down the grassy hill.
I bent my knees up small, took a deep breath
and I was off.
My arms shot out sideways.
I gathered speed.
My eyes squinted.
Sky and grass, dazzle and dark.

I went on forever,
My arms were covered with dents,
holes, squashed grass.
Before I knew it I was at the bottom.
The game was over.
The door of the classroom closed behind me.
I can smell chalk dust, and hear the voice of teacher,
to make me forget my hill.

Andrew Taylor

SPORTS

I'm a Man

I'm a man.
    A grown up man?
A nearly man.
    A man in short trousers?
Short trouser man.
    Can you drive?
I walk to the park.
    A short trouser park keeper?
I'm a goalie.
    And can't touch the bar?
But I'm growing.
    Growing?
Bit by bit.
    A bit on the top?
To reach the bar.
    And a bit on the bottom?
To lengthen into longs.
    And then you'll be a bit of a park-keeper?
No. Then I'll be a goalie.
    In long trousers?
No. In shorts.
    I don't see the point.
Who asked you to?

Michael Rosen

Choosing Sides

First you stand in a bunch
Then it's decided
– though everybody already knows it –
that Rolf and Erik are going to choose
Rolf stands on one line
Erik stands on another
All of us others sit down by the fence
'Lars!' calls out Rolf
'Harold!' yells Erik!
'Emil!' 'Kent!' 'David!' 'Thomas!' 'Martin!'
Then it's only me left;
I go to Erik's team
that's already started dribbling the ball . . .

Siv Widerberg

Here are the Football Results

League Division Fun
Manchester United won, Manchester City lost.
Crystal Palace 2, Buckingham Palace 1
Millwall Leeds nowhere
Wolves 8 A cheese roll and had a cup of tea 2
Aldershot 3 Buffalo Bill shot 2
Evertonill, Liverpool's not very well either
Newcastle's Heaven Sunderland's a very nice place 2
Ipswhich one? You tell me.

Michael Rosen

Football Game

The blue sky
The gold and scarlet shirts
And black shorts
The football match began
Dashing movement
Thrilling, excitement,
Energy, lively,
Whistle, sweat,
Fierce attack
Hopeful,
Spectators cheering,
Bouncing ball
Dashing players
Whistle blows
Half time
Cool refreshments
No score yet
Half hour to go
Back on the field
To sweat and heat
Whistle blows

Off again
Zooming down the field
Goal at last
1–0 and ten minutes
to go
Spectators roaring
Brilliant play
Fierce attack
Whistle blows
Full time
We've won 1–0.

Roger Gibbs (aged 11)

The Pass

I was going like a rocket
When Pearson passed the ball.
I took it really cleanly
And astonished them all.

The last match of the season —
Vital that we score.
But should I pass to Armstrong,
Or go myself 'n make sure?

If I pass to Armstrong
He may drop it — he's a clot.
I'll go myself I reckon —
We need to win a lot.

But there's a massive forward
About to join the fray.
I think I'll pass to Armstrong —
We're bound to win that way.

But just as I made my mind up
And the ball to Armstrong tossed,
The referee blew his whistle,
The game finished, and we lost.

Benjamin Bolt

Cricketer

Light
as the flight
of a bird on the wing
my feet skim the grass
and my heart seems to sing:
'How green is the wicket.
It's cricket.
It's spring.'

Maybe the swallow
high in the air
knows what I feel
when I bowl fast and follow
the ball's twist and bounce.
Maybe the cat
knows what I feel like, holding my bat
and ready to pounce.
Maybe the tree
so supple and yielding
to the wind's sway
then swinging back, gay,
might know the way
I feel when I'm fielding.

Oh, the bird, the cat and the tree:
they're cricket, they're me.

R. C. Scriven

There's a Breathless Hush in the Close Tonight

There's a breathless hush in the Close tonight –
Ten to make and the match to win –
A bumping pitch and a blinding light,
An hour to play and the last man in,
And it's not for the sake of a ribboned coat,
Or the selfish hope of a season's fame,
But his Captain's hand on his shoulder smote –
'Play up! play up! and play the game!'

The sand of the desert is sodden red, –
Red with the wreck of a square that broke; –
The gatling's jammed and the colonel dead,
And the regiment blind with the dust and smoke.
The river of death has brimmed its banks
And England's far and honour a name,
But the voice of a schoolboy rallies the ranks:
'Play up! play up! and play the game!'

Sir Henry Newbolt

I Ran for a Catch

I ran for a catch
    With the sun in my eyes, sir,
Being sure of a 'snatch'
    I ran for a catch . . .
Now I wear a black patch
    And a nose *such* a size, sir,
I ran for a catch
    With the sun in my eyes, sir.

Coulson Kernahan

The Name of the Game

'Catch the *ball*!' the teacher cried.
I ran, I jumped, I stretched, I tried.
I really did.
            – I missed.

'Useless!' she yelled. 'Silly girl!' she spat.
'What on earth d'you think you're playing at?'
'A game,' I said.
            – And wept.

Jenny Craig

Rounders

There once was a boy called Paul
Who couldn't throw a rounders ball.
When trying to throw,
His shoulder said 'No'.
What an awkward shoulder had Paul!

Howard Wilkinson (aged 9)

Games Lesson – Rounders

	Bowl from the bowler.
Batsman:	Whack!
Other fielders:	'Catch!'
	Missed.
	'Stupid, let me go there.'
Teacher:	'One rounder.'
	I feel so hopeless now.

Gail Harding (aged 9)

OUT OF
SCHOOL

Voices

Oh, Cuckoo, Cuckoo away on Knockree,
'Tis well for yourself now you're idle and free,
For there you are gaming away on the hill,
And I'm in the schoolhouse obliged to sit still.
    Is it 'When will you come?'
    When I finish my sum.
    If the clock would strike four
    Then they'll open the door.

Let you call me then, Cuckoo, call out loud and I'll
                           come.
Away in the meadows the corncrakes shout
'Will you come now an' seek me? Come out, come
                           out.
I'm under the window, I'm close to the wall,
I'm holding the wall up for fear it would fall.
    Am I under your feet
    Or away in the wheat?
    Let you seek for me soon;
    I've been calling since noon.'
And it's here I sit working, nigh kilt with the heat.

The king has a right to make it a rule
That only old men should be sitting in school.
I'm moidhered with voices singing and humming,
'The hours are passing and when are you coming?'
    Just a minyit or more
    An' they'll open the door.
    When I've finished my sum
    Be aware! for I'll come.
Och! Now glory to goodness! the clock's striking
                           four!

W. M. Letts

132

School's Out

Girls scream,
    Boys shout;
Dogs bark,
    School's out.

Cats run,
    Horses shy;
Into trees
    Birds fly.

Babes wake
    Open–eyed.
If they can,
    Tramps hide.

Old man,
    Hobble home;
Merry mites,
    Welcome.

W. H. Davies

Out of School

Four o'clock strikes
There's a rising hum,
Then the doors fly open
The children come.

With a wild cat-call
And a hop-scotch hop
And a bouncing ball
And a whirling top.

Grazing of knees
A hair-pull and a slap,
A hitched up satchel,
A pulled down cap,

Bully boys reeling off
Hurt ones squealing off,
Aviators wheeling off,
Mousy ones stealing off,

Woollen gloves for chilblains,
Cotton rags for snufflers,
Pig-tails, coat-tails,
Tails of mufflers.

Machine gun cries
A kennelful of snarlings
A hurricane of leaves
A treeful of starlings,

Thinning away now
By some and some,
Thinning away, away,
All gone home.

Hal Summers

Walking from School

Walking from school is a consummate art:
Which routes to follow to avoid the gangs,
Which paths to find that lead, circuitous,
To leafy squirrel haunts and plopping ponds,
For dreams of Archibald and Tiger Tim;
Which hiding-place is safe, and when it is;
What time to leave to dodge the enemy.
I only once was trapped. I knew the trap –
I heard it in their tones: 'Walk back with us.'
I knew they weren't my friends; but that soft voice
Wheedled me from my route to cold Swain's Lane.
There in a holly bush they threw me down,
Pulled off my shorts, and laughed and ran away;
And, as I struggled up, I saw grey brick,
The cemetery railings, and the tombs.

John Betjeman
(from 'Summoned by Bells')

11 Bus

As usual the old bulky brigade bumbling,
Entered the bus stumbling,
Hands in pockets, moaning and mumbling,
For fare fumbling,
But boys behind them bundling,
With long, straight-laced boots trundling,
Set the fumbling, mumbling, bumbling, tumbling
                        old maids grumbling.
With a sudden hefty whack
The bundling, trundling boys were crumbling,
Before an umbrella.

S. Hale

Top-secret School

Five days a week, except when irksome ears
Or churchyard coughs confine the little dears,

Sealed when it's wet or swaddled when it's cool,
The tots are taken to their Infant School.

Some trudge on leaden feet or lag behind,
Feasting their eyes on slugs and things they find.

Some shoot ahead or steer a curving course,
Claiming to be a capsule or a horse,

But most arrive by car and, having come,
Commingle with a penetrating hum.

MY DAD

Till noon they stay and then they get dismissed
And carted home and, for the most part, kissed,

And, at some point in these affecting scenes,
Changed from their blazers into jodhs or jeans.

What happens in between, what painting pads
They splodge with green-haired mums and noseless
                                                    dads,

What mimes and rhymes and roundelays they try
Or if they simply sit and multiply,

Or play pontoon or plant unceasing cress
Or fly to Mars is anybody's guess.

Brash elders bravely seeking to obtain
Enlightenment on matters in this vein

Find their demands invariably met
With a shrill-giggled 'Golly! I forget.'

                                    Daniel Pettiward

137

After School

Hey little ghostie,
I spy you peeping there.
You thought I didn't see you
Taking the school room air.

Nice little ghostie
In your school pinafore
Neatly darned and ironed
That you always wore.

Pale little ghostie
Standing open–eyed
In the dark half shadow
By the cupboard's side.

Well, little ghostie
Puzzled at what you see?
Blocks, bricks, discs and cubes,
A plastic miscellany.

So little ghostie
Did you chant A – B – C?
Scratch on a squeaky slate
To learn calligraphy?

Poor little ghostie
Did you hold your fingers bent?
Stitching at a sampler?
And catechise for Lent?

Tell, little ghostie
Are children still the same
Jumping to a skipping rhyme?
Was that your favourite game?

Now little ghostie
What did you seek to know
In this tired old school room
From a hundred years ago?

Quiet little ghostie
Creeping without a sound,
Peering, prying slyly –
I don't mind if you're around.

Robert Sparrow

Parents' Evening

Tonight your mum and dad go off to school.
The classroom's empty.
Rabbit and gerbil sleep.
Your painting's with the others on the wall,
And all the projects you have ever done,
The long–since–finished and the just–begun,
Are ranged on desks.
Your books are in a pile.
'He gets his fractions right,' your teacher says.
Your mother reads your 'news',
Is pleased to find you've prominently listed
The sticky pudding that you liked last Tuesday.

Suppose one evening you could go along
To see how mum and dad had spent their days,
What sort of work would you find up on show?
Bus–loads of people,
Towers of coins,
Letters to fill a hundred postmen's sacks,
Hayricks of dust from offices and houses,
Plates, cakes, trains, clothes,
Stretches of motorways and bridges,
Aeroplanes and bits of ships,
Bulldozers and paperclips,
'Cellos and pneumatic drills.
A noise to make the sleepy gerbil stir.

Shirley Toulson

Homework

Homework sits on top of Sunday, squashing
Sunday flat.
Homework has the smell of Monday, homework's
very fat
Heavy books and piles of paper, answers I don't
know.
Sunday evening's almost finished, now I'm going
to go
Do my homework in the kitchen. Maybe just a
snack,
Then I'll sit right down and start as soon as I run
back
For some chocolate sandwich cookies. Then I'll
really do
All that homework in a minute. First I'll see what
new
Show they've got on television in the living room.
Everybody's laughing there, but misery and gloom
And a full refrigerator are where I am at.
I'll just have another sandwich. Homework's very
fat.

Russell Hoban

A Little Mistake

I studied my tables over and over, and backwards
        and forwards, too;
But I couldn't remember six times nine, and I didn't
        know what to do,
Till sister told me to play with my doll, and not to
        bother my head.
'If you call her 'fifty-four' for a while, you'll learn it
        by heart,' she said.

So I took my favourite Mary Ann (though I thought
        'twas a dreadful shame
To give such a perfectly lovely child such a perfectly
        horrid name),
And I called her 'My dear little fifty-four' a hundred
        times, till I knew
The answer of six times nine as well as the answer of
        two times two.

Next day, Elizabeth Wrigglesworth, who always
        acts so proud,
Said 'Six times nine is fifty-two,' and I nearly
        laughed aloud!
But I wished I hadn't when teacher said, 'Now,
        Dorothy, tell if you can.'
For I thought of my doll, and – oh dear, oh dear! – I
        answered 'Mary Ann'!

A. M. Platt

No more days of school,
No more days of sorrow,
No more days of YAK YAK YAK
'Cos we're off tomorrow.

No more pencils, no more books,
No more teacher's ugly looks,
No more things that bring us sorrow
'Cos we won't be here tomorrow.

We break up, we break down,
We don't care if the school falls down.
This time next week where shall we be?
Out of the gates of misery!
No more Latin, no more French,
No more sitting on the hard old bench.
No more cabbages filled with slugs,
No more drinking out of dirty old mugs.
No more spiders in my tea,
Making googly eyes at me.
Kick up tables, kick up chairs,
Kick old teacher down the stairs,
If that does not serve her right,
Blow her up with dynamite.

Saturdays

Real
Genuine
Saturdays
Like marbles
Conkers
Sweet new potatoes
Have their especial season
Are all morning
With midday at five o'clock.
True Saturdays
Are borrowed from early Winter
And the left overs
Of Autumn sunshine days
But separate from days of snow.
The skies dine on dwindles of smoke
Where leafy plots smoulder
With small fires.
Sunday meat is bought
And late
Large, white loaves
From little corner shops.
People passing
Wave over garden walls,
Greengrocers and milkmen are smiled upon
And duly paid.
It is time for the chequered tablecloth
And bowls of soup.
And early on
We set out with some purpose
Through only

Lovely Saturday,
Under skies
Like sun–shot water,
For the leccy train
And the Match in Liverpool.

Gareth Owen

Saturdays

When I was ten, a Saturday
Stretched its barefoot, hungry way
From waking up and hearing Mum
And seeing if the post had come
To breakfast . . . curly bacon . . . then . . .
Begin again
With fried bread central on the plate . . .
Still only half past eight.

Then the long, sweet freedom of the day
For play
And pocket money.
Every Saturday was sunny.

Gwen Dunn

Hymn for Saturday

Now's the time for mirth and play,
Saturday's an holiday;
Praise to heaven unceasing yield,
I've found a lark's nest in the field.

A lark's nest, then your playmate begs
You'd spare herself and speckled eggs;
Soon she shall ascend and sing
Your praises to the eternal King.

Christopher Smart

Sitting on Trev's back wall on the last day of the holidays trying to think of something to do

We sit and squint on Trev's back wall
By the clothes line
Watching the shirts flap
Hearing the shirts slap
In the sunshine.
There's nothing much to do at all
But try to keep cool
And it's our last day
Of the holiday
Tomorrow we're back at school.

We keep suggesting games to play
Like Monopoly.
But you need a day

If you want to play
It properly.
We played for four hours yesterday
Between rainfalls
In Trev's front room
That's like a tomb
And always smells of mothballs.

Says Trev, 'Why don't we kick a ball
Over the Wasteground?'
But the weather's got
Far too hot
To run around.
John kicks his heels against the wall
Stokesy scratches his head
I head a ball
Chalk my name on the wall
While Trev pretends that he's dead.

Says John, 'Let's go to the cinder track
And play speedway.
We can go by the dykes
It's not far on our bikes
I'll lead the way.'
'My saddlebag's all straw at the back
Being used by blackbirds.'
'And there's something unreal
About my fixed wheel
It only drives me backwards.'

Trev's Granny chucks out crusts of bread
For the sparrows
While their black cat

147

Crouches flat
Winking in the shadows.
Trev leaps up and bangs his head
With a sudden roar.
'We could er . . . . .,' he says.
'We could er . . . . .,' he says.
And then sits down once more.

'Let's play Releevo on the sands,'
Says John at last.
We set out with a shout
But his mother calls out,
'It's gone half-past
Your tea's all laid, you wash your hands
They're absolutely grey.'
'Oh go on Mum
Do I have to come
We were just going out to play.'

Old Stokes trails home and pulls a face.
'I'll see you Trev.'
'See you John.'
'See you Trev.'
'See you tonight the usual place.'
'Yes right, all right.'
'Don't forget.'
'You bet.'
'See you then tonight.'
'See you.'
'See you.'
'See
You.'

Gareth Owen

148

The Porter

I'd like to be a porter, and always on the run.
Calling out, 'Stand aside!' and asking leave of none.
Shoving trucks on people's toes, and having
                                          splendid fun;
Slamming all the carriage doors and locking every
                                          one –
And, when they asked to be let in, I'd say, 'It can't
                                          be done.'

    But I wouldn't be a porter if . . .
      The luggage weighed a ton.
        Would you?

C. J. Dennis

The Barber

I'd like to be a barber, and learn to shave and clip,
Calling out, 'Next, please!' and pocketing my tip.
All day you'd hear my scissors going, 'Snip, Snip,
                                          Snip!'
I'd lather people's faces, and their noses I would grip
While I shaved most carefully along the upper lip.

    But I wouldn't be a barber if . . .
      The razor was to slip.
        Would you?

C. J. Dennis

What Would You Like to be When You Grow Up, Little Girl?

I'd like to be a model girl, lithe and long and lean;
I'd like to be a TV star, shining from the screen:

I'd like to be an actress, and strut upon the stage;
I'd like to be a poet, printed on this page:

I'd like to be a busy nurse, smoothing down the
sheets;
I'd like to be an usherette, and show you to your
seats:

I'd like to be a banker, and make a lot of money;
I'd like to be a bee-keeper, and bask on bread and
honey:

I'd like to be a dancer, and dance the disco beat;
I'd like to be a traffic warden, storming down the
street:

I'd like to be a hairdresser, with blower, brush and
comb;
I'd like to be a Romany, the whole wide world to
roam:

I'd like to be an air hostess, and soar across the seas;
I'd like to be a doctor, and dose you when you
sneeze:

I'd like to be in parliament, and speak a speech for
                                                    you
I'd like to be a High Court Judge, and try a case or
                                                    two:

I'd like to be a teacher, and quell you with one look;
I'd like to be an artist, and illustrate this book:

I'd like to be a gymnast, and balance on a bar;
I'd like to be a grand chauffeur, and drive a dashing
                                                    car:

I'd like to be a skater, racing round a rink;
I'd like to be just *anything* . . . I think!

Jenny Craig

151

Career

I'd rather drive an engine than
Be a little gentleman
I'd rather go shunting and hooting
Then hunting and shooting.

Daniel Pettiward

Psychological Prediction

I think little Louie will turn out a crook. He
Puts on rubber gloves when stealing a cookie.

Virginia Brasier

Jobs

Pete wants to be a computer operator
He read about it in a book
But you need to know about
Silicon chips
And scientific gobbledy-gook.

Joe wants to be a footballer
A goalie, a really big star
But you need to like fast cars
And fast women
Whatever they are.

Mike wants to be astronaut
He saw them on the box
But you need to wear them
Goldfish bowls and plastic
Shoes and socks.

But when I'm asked myself, by you
I whistle and look blank
Could I really drive a train
Put out fires or
Sit in a bank?

I don't really want to do anything
I just can't find a niche
Oh, one thing I hadn't thought of
I know what I'll do
I'll teach.

Benjamin Bolt

MORE ^{CH}SKOOL VERSE

Chosen by Jennifer and Graeme Curry

Illustrated by David English

RED FOX

This anthology
is dedicated to DIGGORY, growing up
in his world of books

Contents

GOING TO SCHOOL

Summer Goes

Summer goes, summer goes
Like the sand between my toes
When the waves go out.
That's how summer pulls away,
Leaves me standing here today,
Waiting for the school bus.

Summer brought, summer brought
All the frogs that I have caught,
Frogging at the pond,
Hot dogs, flowers, shells and rocks,
Postcards in my postcard box –
Places far away.

Summer took, Summer took
All the lessons in my book,
Blew them far away.
I forgot the things I knew –
Arithmetic and spelling too,
Never thought about them.

Summer's gone, summer's gone –
Fall and winter coming on,
Frosty in the morning.
Here's the school bus right on time.
I'm not really sad that I'm
Going back to school.

Russell Hoban

The Old School Bus

It takes twenty minutes from my house up the road
For the old school bus to deliver its load.
With its worn out engine and noisy brakes
That's the time it takes,
To talk about last night's telly,
Eat a fruit gum (without chewing),
Do your homework,
Write something rude on the steamed up window,
Or hide Tommy Meacham's satchel so as he won't
   find it
And be late again.

We all hate the bus, but it isn't to blame,
Because even without it we'd go to school just the
   same.
In fact we'd probably have to walk
And then how would we talk,
Or swop sandwiches,
Have bubble gum blowing competitions,
Sing dirty songs,
Or hide Tommy Meacham's satchel so as he won't
   find it
And be late again.

Although it's a curse and a bind and a blow
To wait for the bus in the rain and the snow,
It sometimes seems sad when we look at that bus
To think that one day it will leave without us.

Charles Davies

The Good, the Bored and the Ugly

A coachload of pupils
Get into their places –
The ones in the back seats
Make ugly grimaces.

The ones in the front seats
Are fairer of feature –
Directing the driver
And talking to Teacher.

The ones in the middle –
Halfway down the bus,
Just look bored and wonder,
'Oh, why all the fuss?'

Colin West

First Primrose

I saw it in the lane
One morning going to school
After a soaking night of rain,
the year's first primrose,
Lying there familiar and cool
In its private place
Where little else grows
Beneath dripping hedgerows,
Stalk still wet, face
Pale as Inca gold,
Spring glistening in every delicate fold.
I knelt down by the roadside there,
Caught the faint whiff of its shy scent
On the cold and public air,
Then got up and went
On my slow way,
Glad and grateful I'd seen
The first primrose that day,
Half yellow, half green.

Leonard Clark

The False Knight and The Wee Boy

'O whare are ye gaun?'
  Quo' the fause knicht upon the road:
'I'm gaun to the scule,'
  Quo' the wee boy, and still he stude.

'What is that upon your back?'
  Quo' the fause knicht upon the road:
'Atweel it is my bukes,'
  Quo' the wee boy, and still he stude.

'What's that ye've got in your arm?'
  Quo' the fause knicht upon the road:
'Atweel it is my peit,'
  Quo' the wee boy, and stil he stude.

'Wha's aucht thae sheep?'
  Quo' the fause knicht upon the road:
'They are mine and my mither's,'
  Quo' the wee boy, and still he stude.

'How mony o' them are mine?'
  Quo' the fause knicht upon the road:
'A' they that hae blue tails,'
  Quo' the wee boy, and still he stude.

'I wiss ye were on yon tree,'
  Quo' the fause knicht upon the road:
'And a gude ladder under me,'
  Quo' the wee boy, and still he stude.

'And the ladder for to break,'
  Quo' the fause knicht upon the road:
'And for you to fa' down,'
  Quo' the wee boy, and still he stude.

'I wiss ye were in yon sie,'
    Quo' the fause knicht upon the road:
'And a gude bottom under me,'
    Quo' the wee boy, and still he stude.

'And the bottom for to break,'
    Quo' the fause knicht upon the road:
'And ye to be drowned,'
    Quo' the wee boy, and still he stude.

Anon

It's School Today

I wake up early, it's school today,
I'll get up early and be on my way.
I wash my face, I brush my hair,
I hang my nightdress on the chair.

The breakfast table is all set,
I'll eat it quickly and feed my pet,
I wave to mum and shut the gate;
I'll have to hurry, it's half past eight.
The bus has gone. I'll run to school.
I pass the shops and the swimming pool.
I reach the gate: it's five past nine,
Goodness me! I'm just in time.

Anon

Red Cows

Red cows that line the dusty road,
Along my way to school;
There where the clustered gum-trees shed
A patch of shadowed cool.

You lift your slow, wise heads and stare,
Knee-deep among the grass.
I know you would not harm me; still,
I wish I need not pass.

As I trudge on, with whistled tune,
To keep my courage high,
Your slow, wise heads all gravely turn,
To watch me passing by.

Till, as I reach the bend, and see
The school-house, square and plain,
You drop your slow, wise heads to graze
The shadowed grass again.

Lydia Pender

The Wind

The wind was bringing me to school,
And that is the fast way to get to school.
So why don't you let the wind bring you
To school just like me? And you will be
In school on time, just like I was.

James Snyder (aged 6)

First Day at School

'I am not going!'
My mum grips my hand
Assuring that it's fun.
Suddenly!
Gates stare at me
That are bigger than my dad.
'Do they eat shredded wheat?'
They open
I walk in
Boys run about
Shouting.
A lady walks up.
'Whose mummy are you?' I say.
A bell rings.
Then a whistle blows.
Children walk in a big, big house.
Doors shut like prison gates.
My mummy's hand leaves mine
My last words are...
'Please look after teddy!'

Melanie Louise Skipper (aged 11)

Thinking

Sometimes I think teachers are fed up with me
because I keep forgetting what they say.
Often when they say things I am thinking
about something more important, like today

I am busy thinking out a patent bicycle
to pedal me uphill to school, and back,
with a top to keep the cold and wind and rain out,
a headlight and a proper luggage rack.

My feet and legs got wet again this morning,
my fingers have gone stiff and blueish–white,
my books fell in a filthy oily puddle.
I think I look and feel a proper sight.

'Think of Romans,' he keeps saying,'racing
    chariots…'
but I prefer to think of what it's like
in his nifty purple racer. He's forgotten
I race two miles uphill each day, on a bike.

Jane Whittle

SCHOOL THOUGHTS

School Buses

You'd think that by the end of June they'd take
    themselves
Away, get out of sight – but no, they don't; they
Don't at all. You see them waiting through
July in clumps of sumac near the railroad, or
Behind a service station, watching, always
    watching for a
Child who's let go of summer's hand and strayed. I
    have
Seen them hunting on the roads of August – empty
    buses
Scanning woods and ponds with rows of empty
    eyes. This morning
I saw five of them, parked like a week of
Schooldays, smiling slow in orange paint and
Smirking with their mirrors in sun –
But summer isn't done! Not yet!

Russell Hoban

Impressions of a New Boy

This school is huge – I hate it!
Please take me home.
Steep stairs cut in stone,
Peeling ceiling far too high,
The Head said 'Wait' so I wait alone
Alone though Mum stands here, close by.

The voice is loud – I hate it!
Please take me home.

170

'Come. Sit. What is your name?'
Trembling lips. The words won't come.
The Head says 'Speak,' but my cheeks flame,
I hear him give a quiet sigh.

The room is full – I hate it
Please take me home.

A sea of faces stare at me,
My desk is much too small,
Its wooden ridge rubs my knee,
But Head said 'Sit' so though I'm tall
I know that I must try.

The yard is full – I hate it,
Please take me home.

Bodies jostle me away,
Pressing me against the wall.
Then one boy says, 'Want to play?'
The boy says, 'Catch' and throws a ball,
And playtime seems to fly.

This school is great – I love it.

Marian Collihole

First Day at School

My first day at school today.
Funny sort of day.
Didn't seem to learn much.
Seemed all we did was play.
Then teacher wrote some letters
On a board all painted black
And then we had a story and ...
I don't think I'll go back.

Rod Hull

This 'Ere School

This 'ere school is filthy,
This 'ere school is cold,
This 'ere school is full of rules –
Made for five year olds.

These 'ere teachers are boring,
I wonder if they're able –
To write non-stop an essay
Or to say by heart a fable?

This 'ere school's got children
Laughing by a wall
Maybe this 'ere school
Ain't so bad after all.

Stephanie Marshall (aged 14)

I Don't want to go to School Today

I don't want to go to school today,
'Cos I hate it,
'Cos it's Maths,
'Cos it's History,
'Cos it's being told off,
'Cos it's anything.

I *might* go to school today,
'Cos it's alright,
'Cos it's Woodwork,
'Cos it's Football,
'Cos it's Friday,
'Cos it's… OK.

I think I *will* go to school today,
'Cos there's chips,
'Cos there's films,
'Cos there's my mates,
'Cos she sits in the row in front,
'Cos she smiled at me.

Christopher Mann

The School

The houses are red and tall or small
With brown birds perched on the backyard wall.
The school where I work and play each day
Is made of stone and old and grey,
And rain can't wash away the soot
That covers it from head to foot.
It's full as a parcel of girls and boys,
Drawings, paintings, writing, toys,
Dinners, teachers, pets and noise.

Stanley Cook

Sounds of School

The footsteps of a running boy,
The rumble of traffic,
The deep voice of a teacher,
The babble of voices from another classroom,
The creak of a desk,
The click as a pen or pencil is put down on a desk,
The slither of paper, sliding across a desk,
The high–pitched sound of chalk being used on a
    blackboard.

Timothy Hearn

On a March Morning

A smell of warmth in the air,
A sea of books in the library,
The buzz of conversation,
Shouts of glee from a PE class,
The echo of feet running through the corridors,
The beginnings of bean plants,
A smell of burning,
Sleepy cars resting in the car park,
Tapping of the gardener's hammer,
Dewy grass scattered with daisies like snowflakes,
The remains of an orange scattered round a bin,
The beginnings of a currant pudding ...
Fish mobiles hanging from the ceiling,
Faces painted and stuck on the wall,

Mrs Newman is teaching English,
A sea with ships,
'Finishing off' time,
Mrs Sequeire teaching maths,
The beginning of an icy picture,
Mrs Saxon teaching reading,
Pictures of faces and monsters,
Miss Sumpster teaching writing,
Bird mobiles hanging from the ceiling,
Poetry and pictures,
Paper men and women hanging from the wall,
Mr Smith teaching geometry,
Drawing circles and shapes,
And a weasel and a stoat stuffed and on show.

Jacqueline Davis (aged 10)

Go Away and Shut Up

I asked my Dad why I had to be quiet
He said
   'Go away and shut up.'
I asked my Mum why I couldn't fly my
Kite she said
   'Go away and shut up.'
I asked my friend why I couldn't
Play with her she said
   'Go away and shut up.'
I knocked on the staffroom door and
Asked for Sir he said
   'Go away and shut up.'
I asked myself why everyone was
Saying
   'Go away and shut up.'
But no answer came all I heard
Was
   'GO AWAY AND SHUT UP.'

Colleen Boland (aged 10)

Oh bring back higher standards

Oh bring back higher standards –
the pencil and the cane –
if we want education then we must have some pain.
Oh, bring us back all the gone days
Yes, bring back all the past . . .
let's put them all in rows again – so we can see who's
   last.

Let's label all the good ones
(the ones like you and me)
and make them into prefects – like prefects used to
    be.
We'll put them on the honours board
. . . as honours ought to be,
and write their names in burnished script –
for all the world to see.
We'll have them back in uniform,
we'll have them doff their caps,
and learn what manners really are
. . . for decent kind of chaps!
. . . So let's label all the good ones,
we'll call them 'A's and 'B's –
and we'll parcel up the useless ones
and call them 'C's and 'D's.
. . . We'll even have an 'E' lot!
. . . an 'F' or 'G' maybe!!
. . . so they can know they're useless,
. . . and not as good as me.

For we've go to have the stupid –
And we've got to have the poor
Because –
        if we don't have them . . .
        well . . . what are prefects for?

Peter Dixon

177

The Magician

From my classroom window I can see a scrap-yard
where the cars are piled on top of each other
like souls in purgatory,
they are the dis-assembling dreams of panel-beaters.
Only a broken fence and a gate hanging
on the gibbet of a single hinge
separate them from their landscape
of broken, churned-up grass
where gipsies' horses and iron wheels
walked yesterday.
Then there are the shacks where the dogs are
    tethered,
barking and crazy all day,
and an enclosure for hens
where the birds run senseless in the pelting rain,
and skirting it all
the dull backs of terraced houses
with their broken chimney cowls and bins,
and the rain, the incessant rain, beating like a
    timpany
on the roofs of the cars and splashing like
    acupuncture
in the puddled field.

And there is a man's pigeon loft:
I think he is a magician,
for every morning as he walks on this sea of
    wreckage,
the rain stops, the grass seems to stiffen, the roof-
    tops glisten,
and even the cars take on that frozen intensity
of still life after rain.
The man lifts his arm,
the sun rises,
the loft door opens
and a hundred swirling, tumbling acrobats cascade
and dance
in the dismal air.
And other birds squawk and cry and reel, magpies,
    pee-wits,
seagulls, far from the coast, attracted by the water,
    climb
and build around the column of the sun.

The man lowers his arm
and bows to me.
The children stare at him –
they can see that he has changed a landscape
which their teacher thought was ugly
into the trappings of music, and the movement of
                 wings.

Shaun Traynor

I Don't Know

I am sitting here, trying to think,
Trying to think of a poem.
Mr Bell says to me 'What are you going to write
    about?'
I don't know.

I am sitting here trying to think,
Trying to think of a poem.
My friends have done a page but I've done nothing.
I don't know.

I am sitting here, trying to think,
Trying to think of a poem.
Mr Bell says 'I will be very angry if you haven't
    done anything.'
I don't know.

I am sitting here, trying to think,
Trying to think of a poem.
Mr Bell's coming round. 'That's good,' says Mr
    Bell.
I looked at the page and it was full of a poem called –
I Don't Know.

Mhairi Boyle (age 10)

180

Red Ink

The day I borrowed Miss Ward's red ink,
I'd nearly opened it and she gave me a wink.
'Don't open it,' she said to me,
I wondered why, so I thought I'd see.
I opened the bottle as slowly as I could,
I was nearly there, and I wondered if I should.
I was so curious of what was inside,
When I opened it I nearly died.
Oh why Miss Ward did you give me a wink?
Because in the bottle was. . . normal red ink.

Sarah Rogers (age 10)

The Computer
(A Pantoum)

A Pantoum is a verse form from south-east Asia.

We've got a computer at school,
we use it when teachers are out,
we know it's A TECHNICAL TOOL
which is what OUR GREAT FUTURE's about.

We use it when teachers are out
to PLAY all THE GAMES we enjoy
which is what OUR GREAT FUTURE's about.
We will need every NEW KIND OF TOY.

To PLAY all THE GAMES we enjoy
when we leave school to LEAD OUR OWN LIVES
we will need every NEW KIND OF TOY.
THE ONE WHO LEARNS FASTEST SURVIVES.

When we leave school to LEAD OUR OWN LIVES
computers will CUT DOWN THE LABOUR.
THE ONE WHO LEARNS FASTEST SURVIVES
to look after THE BEGGAR MY NEIGHBOUR.

Computers will CUT DOWN THE LABOUR,
THE PEOPLE who use them WILL RULE
to look after THE BEGGAR MY NEIGHBOUR.
We've got a computer at school.

Jane Whittle

SCHOOL PUPILS

Ten Little Schoolboys

Ten little schoolboys went out to dine;
One choked his little self, and then there were nine.

Nine little schoolboys sat up very late;
One overslept himself, and then there were eight.

Eight little schoolboys travelling to Devon;
One said he'd stay there, and then there were seven.

Seven little schoolboys chopping up sticks;
One chopped himself in half and then there were
    six.

Six little schoolboys playing with a hive;
A bumble bee stung one, and then there were five.

Five little schoolboys going in for law;
One got in chancery, and then there were four.

Four little schoolboys going out to sea,
A red herring swallowed one, and then there were
    three.

Three little schoolboys walking in the zoo;
A big bear hugged one, and then there were two.

Two little schoolboys sitting in the sun;
One got frizzled up, and then there was one.

One little schoolboy living all alone;
He got married, and then there was none.

Anon

Johnson Broke my Ruler, Sir

Johnson broke my ruler, sir,
He did, sir, honest;
Johnson broke my ruler, sir;
Please sir, that's not fair!

Johnson did it *twice,* sir;
He did, sir, honest:
Johnson did it *twice,* sir,
Please sir, he *did*!

Can't you make him stop it, sir?
Please sir, please?
Can't you make him stop it, sir?
I didn't do a thing!

Why's it me that's punished, sir?
Why, sir, why?
Why's it me that's punished, sir?
I only got him back.

Please don't tell my Dad, sir;
Please don't, please;
Please don't tell my Dad, sir;.
I won't do that again.

Johnson had it coming, sir;
Please sir, he did.
Johnson had it coming, sir;
(Stupid little kid).

Christopher Mann

The Fight

I remember, when we were just nippers,
Michael Saunders and I were sworn foes;
One morning of sunlit September
It looked as though we'd come to blows.

At playtime, quite close to the railings,
Out of sight from our teacher, Miss Bee,
I threatened that awful boy, Saunders,
And he in his turn threatened me.

He said that he'd tear me to ribbons.
'You and whose army?' I said.
(We were terribly witty in those days.)
I told him I'd kick in his head.

We circled each other like panthers
(Out of range of each other, of course);
We glared at each other like tigers,
Observed by the greengrocer's horse.

A little crowd gathered around us;
They egged us both on to begin.
Kathy Woodward (who wetted her knickers)
Said she'd notify our next-of-kin.

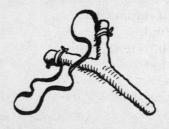

Someone pushed me towards Michael Saunders;
Thank God, he stepped out of the way.
We started to take off our jackets . . .
A Spitfire, it was, saved the day.

Overhead, the Battle of Britain
Was beginning in earnest once more;
Like tigers and panthers, the aircraft
Were trying to settle the score.

They spat at each other with bullets;
When two of them fell in their flames
Miss Bee led us all to the shelters
To play mental arithmetic games.

Sometimes I see Michael Saunders
In the pub of a Saturday night.
Forty years have elapsed since that morning
When two little boys had a fight:

But Michael still often reminds me
Of that day. What he always says is:
'I bet you my Dad could beat your Dad.'
And I tell him that mine could beat his.

We play cards in the cosy bar-parlour,
Our glasses of beer side by side;
In the grate a brisk log-fire is burning;
We forget that it's winter outside

Where, in the adjacent graveyard,
Two pilots lie under the snow.
I wonder if Michael or I might have won:
But that's something that we'll never know.

Ted Walker

The Rebel Child

Most days when I
Go off to school
I'm perfectly contented
To follow the rule,

Enjoy my history,
My music, my sums,
Feel a little sorry
When home time comes.

But on blowabout mornings
When clouds are wild
And the weather in a tumult –
I'm a rebel child.

I sit quite calmly,
My face at rest,
Seem quite peaceable,
Behave my best;

But deep inside me
I'm wild as a cloud,
Glad the sky is thrown about
Glad the storm's loud!

And when school's over
And I'm out at last,
I'll laugh in the rain,
Hold my face to the blast,

Be free as the weather,
Bellow and shout,
As I run through all the puddles –
'School's out! School's out!'

Leslie Norris

Playing Truant

Davy
was no fan
of the School Attendance man

Maybe
canes and schools
aren't really suitable for fools

the Law
still demanded
that school should be attended

what's more
the Headmaster
proclaimed him a disaster

being no
great bookworm
his liking for lessons was lukewarm

even so he was fluent
in the art of playing truant

Raymond Wilson

The Leader

I wanna be the leader
I wanna be the leader
Can I be the leader?
Can I? I can?
Promise? Promise?
Yippee, I'm the leader
I'm the leader

OK what shall we do?

Roger McGough

When I was lonely

Once we were all friends,
But day after day they left people out.
Monday it was me,
Nobody to play with,
Stamping my feet on the floor,
Kicking the stones about the playground,
Standing against the wall,
Sitting on my own at dinner time,
Surrounded by boys.
Bell goes, nobody to walk home with,
My head sinks to my chest.
The journey home seemed a long way.
Today.

Teresa Steele (aged 11)

The Loner

He leans against the playground wall,
Smacks his hands against the bricks
And other boredom–beating tricks,
Traces patterns with his feet,
Scuffs to make the tarmac squeak,
Back against the wall he stays –
And never plays.

The playground's quick with life,
The beat is strong.
Though sharp as a knife
Strife doesn't last long.
There is shouting, laughter, song,
And a place at the wall
For who won't belong.

We pass him running, skipping, walking,
In slow huddled groups, low talking.
Each in our familiar clique
We pass him by and never speak,
His loneness is his shell and shield
And neither he nor we will yield.

He wasn't there at the wall today,
Someone said he'd moved away
To another school and place
And on the wall where he used to lean
Someone had chalked
'watch this space'.

Julie Holder

Us Dreads

In a dis ya skool
us dreads rool.
Soul head dem saaf
mek us dreads laugh
dem no no how fe dress
but us dreads strickly de bess.
Gal dem cool an
control dem part ah de skool.
Mek us dreads feel sweet
each day ah de week.
Teachars all weird
mek saaf buoy scared
but us dread move together
an control de skool.
De music we play
nice up de day.
Rythdym just nice it
Teachar dem no like it.
When exam come
some dreads run
dem carn do dem tings.
In de enn teachar dem win.
Us dreads carn get na wok
we strickly brok
lose out in de enn
but us dreads still frienn.

Dave Martin

I am a Deemmun

Im a deemmun
I dont no how to spel
I allwaze deay–dreem
and teechuz pik on mi
cos I dont kno how to reed
I dont kair wot pepel sai
I dont nead to reed or ryte
I am not goeng to chooz it in the
therd yeers an
I dont nede it in my Jobb –
Soh thair!
Whot do I kare!

Julia Ignatiou

The Bully

'Where do you live?' the bully said.
'I'll not tell you,' said I.
'Tell me or I'll bash you up,'
But I did not reply.
He advanced on me, his fist upraised;
I stood firmly on my feet.
Then he punched me on the nose
So I said, '23 Albert Street.'

Rod Hull

Thug

School began it.
There he felt
the tongue's salt lash
raising its welt

on a child's heart.
Ten years ruled
by violence left him
thoroughly schooled,

nor did he fail
to understand
the blow of the
headmaster's hand.

That hand his hand
round the cosh curled.
What rules the classroom
rocks the world.

Raymond Garlick

The Bully

There is a boy in our class,
Who makes me blooming sick,
If I thought he wouldn't belt me,
I'd tell him he was thick.

He thinks he's very clever,
Always looking for a fight,
One of these days I'll bash him,
Then run away in fright.

When I grow one inch taller,
I'll hit him on the nose,
That is unless he acts quite smart,
And stands up on his toes.

I hate his ugly face,
I hate the little blighter,
I'd hit him in his weak spot,
If I was a better fighter.

Paul Dingle

Dumb Insolence

I'm big for ten years old
Maybe that's why they get at me

Teachers, parents, cops
Always getting at me

When they get at me

I don't hit em
They can do you for that

I don't swear at em
They can do you for that

I stick my hands in my pockets
And stare at them

And while I stare at them
I think about sick

They call it dumb insolence

They don't like it
But they can't do you for it

I've been done before
They say if I get done again

They'll put me in a home
So I do dumb insolence

Adrian Mitchell

That's Me

Everything that happened that morning is so clear
   to me,
Although it was all three months ago.
'Will you be all right, mum – you don't seem well?'
'Yes, off to school like a good girl.'
But I don't understand decimals this morning.
I don't want to change my library book,
   and yet I love reading.
Must I go to the swimming-baths this afternoon?
Although I know I'm nearly ready for my green
   braid.
   I want to go *home*.
The four o'clock bell,
I race up the road until my breath heaves in my
   throat.
Near home I dawdle, linger, drag –
I can hear my own heart
   and my own footsteps.
A rush of speed up the path –
   a dash at the door –
Dad's smiling face meets me,
His laughing voice tells me I have a new brother.
'You're the eldest, you choose his name.'

The eldest! the big sister!
   That's ME.

Julie Andrews

A Stomach-ache is Worse
Away from Home

'Sir,' I said,
Hoping for sympathy,
'I've got the stomach-ache.'
All of it was true,
There was no putting it on.
I gave out winces with my mouth
Using my eyebrows skilfully
And held the hurt place hard
With both hands.
But it was my white face convinced him.
So he sent me outside
To walk it away in the fresh air.
Outside it was deathly cold.
Because he had his hand up first
Trev came out too
To see I was all right.
A grey wind with rain in it
Whipped across the playground,
Spattering through puddles
And setting the empties rolling
Up and down, up and down
And clatter-rattling in their crates.
Trev said, 'You'll be alright.'
And started kicking a tennis ball
Up against the toilet wall,
His hands in his pockets,
Bent against the cold.

The dinner ladies came out.
Moaning slightly I bent over
And gritted my teeth bravely.
But they didn't see
And walked through the school gates laughing.
At home there would be the smell of cooking
And our Robbo asleep before the fire.
I looked through the railings
And thought my way to our house.
Past the crumbling wall,
The Bingo Hall,
The scraggy tree
As thin as me,
The rotting boarding
By the cinema
With last week's star
In a Yankee car
Flapping on the hoarding.
Stop!
Turn right towards town
And three doors down,
That's our house.

Gareth Owen

The Lesson

'Your father's gone,' my bald headmaster said.
His shiny dome and brown tobacco jar
Splintered at once in tears. It wasn't grief.
I cried for knowledge which was bitterer
Than any grief. For there and then I knew
That grief has uses – that a father dead
Could bind a bully's fist a week or two;
And then I cried for shame, then for relief.

I was a month past ten when I learnt this:
I still remember how the noise was stilled
In school–assembly when my grief came in.
Some goldfish in a bowl quietly sculled
Around their shining prison on its shelf.
They were indifferent. All the other eyes
Were turned towards me. Somewhere in myself
Pride, like a goldfish, flashed a sudden fin.

Edward Lucie-Smith

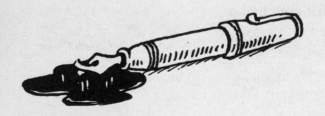

Schoolboy

Oh yes, I remember him well, the boy you are
    searching for;
he looked like most boys, no better, brighter, or
    more respectful;
he cribbed, mitched, spilt ink, rattled his desk and
garbled his lessons, with the worst of them;
he could smudge, hedge, smirk, wriggle, wince,
whimper, blarney, badger, blush, deceive, be
devious, stammer, improvise, assume
offended dignity or righteous indignation as though
    to the manner born;
sullenly and reluctantly he drilled, for some small
crime, under Sergeant Bird, so wittily nicknamed
Oiseau, on Wednesday half-holidays,
appeared regularly in detention classes,
hid in the cloakroom during algebra,
was, when a newcomer, thrown into the bushes of
    the
Lower Playground by bigger boys,
and threw newcomers into the bushes of the Lower
Playground when he was a bigger boy;
he scuffled at prayers,
he interpolated, smugly, the time-honoured wrong
irreverent words into the morning hymns,
he helped to damage the headmaster's rhubarb,
was thirty-third in trigonometry,
and, as might be expected, edited the School
    Magazine.

Dylan Thomas

The Bionic Boy

It really fills me full of joy
To be the first bionic boy;
To know that I have got the power
To run at sixty miles an hour,
To punch my way through doors and walls,
To juggle with three cannon-balls,
To rope a steer or buffalo,
To tie a steel rod in a bow,
To uproot trees, break out of jails,
To fight successfully with whales,
To stop the traffic in the Strand
By waving my bionic hand,
To swim to Cap Gris-Nez and back
And then lay low the whole Welsh pack.
There's just one thing I must explain,
I haven't a bionic brain;
A matter of profound regret,
For I've no 'O'-levels as yet.

Charles Connell

Tom's Bomb

There was a boy whose name was Tom,
Who made a high explosive bomb,
By mixing up some iodine
With sugar, flour and plasticine.
Then, to make it smell more queer,
He added Daddy's home-made beer.
He took it off to school one day,
And when they all went out to play,
He left it by the radiator.

As the heat was getting greater,
The mixture in the bomb grew thick
And very soon it seemed to tick.
Miss Knight came in and gazed with awe
To see the bomb upon the floor.
'Dear me,' she said, 'it is a bomb,
An object worth escaping from.'
She went to Mr. Holliday
And said in tones that were not gay,
'Headmaster, this is not much fun;
There is a bomb in Classroom One.'
'Great snakes,' said he, and gave a cough
And said, 'I hope it won't go off.
But on the off-chance that it does,
I think we'd better call the fuzz.'
A policeman came and said, 'Oh God,
We need the bomb disposal squad,
Some firemen and a doctor too,
A helicopter and its crew,
And, since I'm shaking in the legs,
A pot of tea and hard-boiled eggs.'
A bomb disposal engineer
Said, with every sign of fear,
'I've not seen one like that before,'
And rushed out, screaming, through the door.
Everyone became more worried
Till Tom, who seemed to be unflurried,
Asked what was all the fuss about?
'I'll pick it up and take it out.'
He tipped the contents down the drain
And peace and quiet reigned again.
Tom just smiled and shook his head
And quietly to himself he said:
'Excitement's what these people seek.
I'll bring another one next week.'

David Hornsby

Government Health Warning

The boy stood on the burning desk,
Whence all but he had fled,
He tried to quench the flames with ink
(Which happened to be red);

The fire brigade came rushing round,
With ladders, hose and men:
They tried to reach the stricken lad
But flames roared up again.

'Oh help me, please, Oh help me!
He cried in grief and pain;
'Just get me out; I promise you
I'll never smoke again!'

The firemen they came running
And grabbed the little fool:
And soon he stood there safe and sound
Outside the blazing school.

His friends all gathered round and said:
'Thank God you're in one piece!
We thought they'd never get you out!
Will wonders never cease?'

But then a look of horror ran
Across the young lad's brow;
'I've left a pack of Marlboros there
I don't half need one now!'

Before the watchers scarce could move
Or even cry in fright;
He dashed into the flames again,
And vanished from their sight.

The flames leapt up, and caught the roof,
And down in dust it fell:
And never did they see again
The boy whose tale I tell.

So heed my words, and listen well
If you would live in wealth:
For smoking isn't just a joke.
It *damages* your health!

Christopher Mann

Lizzie

When we went over the park
Sunday mornings
We picked up sides

Lizzie was our centre-forward
Because she had the best shot.

When the teachers
Chose the school team
Marshie was our centre-forward.

Lizzie wasn't allowed to play,
They said.

So she watched us lose, instead.

Michael Rosen

Big Jim

When we play cricket, we don't let Jim bowl;
And when we play baseball, we don't let Jim bat.
But when we play football, we put Jim in goal,
For balls can't get past him, because Jim's so fat.

Colin West

The Changeling

Mary's mother is tall and fair,
Her father is freckled with ginger hair,
And they live in a house all polished and neat
In the very centre of Riverside Street.

But Mary is dark and thin and wild,
And she doesn't laugh like a human child,
And she doesn't cry like you and me
With tears as salt as the brooding sea.

For when Mary giggles the rattling sound
Is worse than the traffic for miles around;
And the sobs that heave Mary's shoulders high,
Leave her throat parched and her wide eyes dry.

In the classroom Mary works on her own,
And she plays in the playground quite alone.
In church she will not pray or sing,
For she never will join in anything.

It can only be that ten years ago,
In hurtling sleet and blinding snow,
Some dreaming wizards or spiteful elves
Went cradle-swapping to please themselves,

Took the real Mary to join their race
And left their fledgeling, in her place,
To grow both beautiful and sly
With power to destroy in her evil eye.

And the only thing both Marys share
Is that they are homesick everywhere.
So sumptuously by the fairies fed,
The one is hungry for human bread.

The other however the heat's turned higher
Is cold for the lack of fairy fire.
And the parents cannot know what is meant
By their daughter's waspish discontent.

Her sulks and tempers are never done,
She's a stock of harsh words for everyone;
While they, dismayed by their puzzling fate,
Go to bed early and get up late.

So now the mother is bent and grey,
And the father sits in his chair all day,
And Riverside Street cannot abide
The slum that their house has become inside.

Shirley Toulson

LESSONS

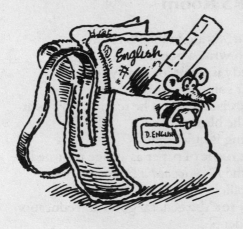

Riddle

I have no voice and yet I speak to you,
I tell of all things in the world that people do;
I have leaves, but I am not a tree,
I have pages, but I am not a bride or royalty;
I have spine and hinges, but I am not a man or a
    door,
I have told you all. I cannot tell you more.

John Cunliffe

Answer: A book

★ The PS Room

Here I am, sitting in the PS room,
Trying to write a poem.
Everybody is silent, or nearly so.
I can hear someone whispering.
Someone else laughs. The teacher frowns at
him and he blushes.
Everything is quiet again.
Only the rustle of paper as a page is turned.
I notice the *Encyclopaedia Britannica* has
been installed,
Probably for 'the general good and education
of all students'.
I flick through one volume and read
the history of the motor–cycle.
Bored, I put it back on the shelf,
Filling in the hole I had made.

Anthony Halliwell

★PS stands for Physical Science

Lmntl

'Albert, have you a turtle?'
I'll say to him, and Bert'll
say 'Yes! Of *course* I have a turtle.'

But if I write
'Have you a trtl, Albert?'
(as I might)
I wonder if Brtl guess
just what I mean?

We all have seen
a dog's tail wagl,
haven't we?
We all agree
that what a dogldo,
a polywogl too.

We've hrd a brd, grls gigl;
observed how skwrls hnt
for nuts; how big pigs grnt;
know how we feel
on hearing young pigsqweel.

Bbbbs buzz, and ktns play;
bats flitrfly azootowls cry.

Why don't we *spell* that way?
Make ibx look like gnu?
Lfnts too; zbras inizoo?
I do. Do you?

David McCord

Write a Poem

'Write a poem,' our teacher said.
'A poem about an animal or place,
Something that has happened to you
In the holidays.
Better still, write about yourself,
What you feel like,
What's inside you
And wants to come out.'
Stephen straight away
Began to write slowly
And went on and on
Without looking up.
John sighed and looked far away
Then suddenly snatched up his pen
And was scribbling and scribbling.
Ann tossed back her long hair
And smiled as she began.
But I sat still.
I thought of fighting cats
With chewed ears
And dogs sniffing their way along
Windy streets strewn with paper
But there seemed nothing new
To say about them . . .
The holidays? Nothing much happened.
And what's inside me?
Only the numbness of cold fingers,
The grey of the sky today.
John sighed again.
Peter coughed.
Papers rustled.
Pens scratched.

A blowfly was fuzzing
At a window pane.
The tittering clock
Kept snatching the minutes away,
I had nothing to say.

Olive Dunn

Riddle

We are very little creatures
All of different voice and features;
One of us in glAss is set,
One of us you'll find in jEt,
T'other you may see in tIn,
And the fourth a bOx within,
If the fifth you would pursue,
It can never fly from yoU.

Jonathan Swift

Answer: The vowels

Schoolpoem 2

One day i went into the school library and
    there were no books. Panic-stricken
i looked for explanations in the eyes
    of a school-tied librarian but
she just stamped a date on my wrist
    and said i was overdue.
Then i spied one little book called
    'HOW TO SPELL'
        but
i new how to do that already,
so i sat feeling pretty lonely
as you can imagine in a bookless library,
    in the skeleton of a library,
going over all the names of books i once new:
    WAR AND PEACE
    DANNY THE DORMOUSE
    how nice and neat and safe they were.
    Now all i do is look for answers
        in my blazer pockets but
    they have gone through the holes
        made by yesterday's
            marbles.

Brian McCabe

214

Arithmetic

I'm 11. And I don't really know
my Two Times Table. Teacher says it's disgraceful
But even if I had the time, I feel too tired.
Ron's 5, Samantha's 3, Carole's 18 months,
and then there's Baby. I do what's required.

Mum's working. Dad's away. And so
I dress them, give them breakfast. Mrs Russell
moves in, and I take Ron to school.
Miss Eames calls me an old-fashioned word: Dunce.
Doreen Maloney says I'm a fool.

After tea, to the Rec. Pram-pushing's slow
but on fine days it's a good place, full
of larky boys. When 6 shows on the clock
I put the kids to bed. I'm free for once.
At about 7 – Mum's key in the lock.

Gavin Ewart

Six Times One

Is six times one a lot of fun?
Or eight times two?
Perhaps for you.
But five times three
Unhinges me,
While six and seven and eight times eight
Put me in an awful state
And four and six and nine times nine
Make me want to cry and whine
So when I get to twelve times ten
I begin to wonder when
I can take a vacation from multiplication
And go out
And start playing again.

Karla Kuskin

In the Garden

Twice one are two,
Violets white and blue.

Twice two are four,
Sunflowers at the door.

Twice three are six,
Sweet peas on their sticks.

Twice four are eight,
Poppies at the gate.

Twice five are ten,
Pansies bloom again.

Twice six are twelve,
Pinks for those who delve.

Twice seven are fourteen,
Flowers of the runner bean.

Twice eight are sixteen,
Clinging ivy ever green.

Twice nine are eighteen,
Purple thistles to be seen.

Twice ten are twenty,
Hollyhocks in plenty.

Twice eleven are twenty-two,
Daisies wet with morning dew.

Twice twelve are twenty-four,
Roses, who could ask for more.

Anon

The Painful Way to Multiply

The teacher viewed the infant boy
Without the slightest sense of joy,
For still he could not calculate
The simple sum of six times eight.

The teacher ranted angrily,
Then took the lad across his knee
And vowed to teach him with a cane
The way to multiply, with pain.

He gave the boy
   six of the best,
But would not let
   the matter rest,
And beat him six times
   more and then
He beat him six times
   once again.

And thus, in multiples
   of six,
Between the pupil's
   cries and kicks,
The teacher could well
   demonstrate
That six times eight
   is forty-eight.

Colin West

1 × 2 is 2

1 × 2 is 2
2 × 2 are 4
3 × 2 are 9
4 × 2 are 17
5 × 2 are 26
6 × 2 are 39
7 × 2 are 148
8 × 2 are 2,204
9 × 2 are 330,916
10 × 2 are 999,999
11 × 2 are 5,222,506½
12 × 2 are 135,926,201⅞

and if anyone says it isn't
meet me in the play ground
tomorrow at high noon,
and don't be late!...

Paul Johnson

Hullo, Inside

Physical–education slides
Show us shots of our insides.
Every day I pat my skin,
'Thanks for keeping it all in.'

Max Fatchen

Science

Science is a world of fun,
They tell me it's a joy;
Explaining all the universe
To every girl and boy.

Zinc Hydroxide, Sodium Chloride, Protons,
    Photons, Quartz!
With names like these to conjure with, who needs
    thoughts?

I've studied all the elements
From arsenic to zinc;
But when it comes to using them
My brain goes on the blink.

Zinc Hydroxide, Sodium Chloride, Napthalene
    and Lime;
Manganese Bromide, Silver Halide, it gets worse all
    the time!

The teachers ask me questions,
'How much, how far, and when?'
I wish they'd try the simple ones
like 'What's fifteen and ten?'

Zinc Hydroxide, Sodium Chloride, Hydrogen and
    Chrome;
If this is what it's leading to I'd rather stay at home.

I've played around with bunsen flames
And test tubes and retorts,
I've mixed up moles and molecules
Of eighty different sorts.

Zinc Hydroxide, Sodium Chloride, Rheostats and
  Pi,
I suppose I should be doing this but I really don't
  know why!

I've tested reactivities
Of Gallium and Tin;
But I still can't quite figure out
What caused the mess I'm in.

Carbon Monoxide, Sodium Fluoride, Mercury and
  Lead;
I wonder why this Science gives me such an aching
  head?

Christopher Mann

A Survey of Sovereigns

William, William, Henry the First,
Stephen and Henry the Second;

Richard and John, sir, and Henry the Third,
Then one, two, three Edwards, 'tis reckoned.

Richard the Second and Henry the Fourth,
And Henrys the Fifth and the Sixth, sir;

Edward the Fourth and young Edward the Fifth,
Then Richard or Crooked King Dick, sir.

Henry the Seventh and Henry the Eighth,
Then Edward, then Mary was queen, sir.

Elizabeth, James, then Kings Charles One and
    Two,
(With Oliver Cromwell between, sir).

James, William & Mary, then following Anne,
Four Georges, one after another;

Then William, Victoria, Edward and George
To Edward, who said, 'Crown my brother.'

Colin West

The School at the Top of the Tree

Mr Beecher, the history teacher,
Kept his school at the top of a tree.
The children came from miles around
For his lessons were fun and his classes were free.

Mr Beecher, the history teacher,
Told them tales of battles long done,
Of kings and princes, in war and peace,
Great glories the world had known.

As they listened and dreamed, through the green,
   leafy days,
Swaying in the summer sun,
Brave heroes haunted the top of the tree –
They loved them, every one;

Poor Harold dead with an arrow in his eye,
Lord Nelson ruling the waves,
Joan of Arc, with her heart on fire,
Wilberforce freeing the slaves.

Mr Beecher, the history teacher,
Had stories to suit every mood.
But the winds sprang up and the leaves whirled high
As winter stalked through the wood.

Then all who heard his golden tongue
Were the forest creatures wild,
A frozen crow and a long-legged hare –
And one last starving child.

Mr. Beecher, the history teacher,
Climbed down from the top of his tree,
Held out his hand to that cold little boy –
And took him home to tea.

Jenny Craig

Millicent and the Nature Ramble

Millicent Mary liked going to school
For her teachers were really quite nice.
They made lessons pleasant, sometimes even fun,
Except Mr Oliver Price.
He was, truth to tell, a peculiar chap
With a passion for ancient Greek culture
And with his hunched back and his bald, bony head,
He looked like an under-fed vulture.

If Milly was mentioned by one of the staff
He would raise up his eyebrows and groan,
Appealing to heaven to spare him this child
Who seemed to be accident prone.
One has to confess, Mr Price had a point,
And one day he even resolved
To hang out the flags when some mishap occurred
In which Milly wasn't involved.

One day the headmaster announced to the school
That plans had been made to arrange
A nature trail ramble for Millicent's class,
He was sure they would welcome the change.
Mother Nature, he said, could be seen at first hand
They could learn from the country at large
But cries of excitement were very soon stilled
When he said Mr Price was in charge.

On the evening preceding the day of the walk
While playing outside on her swing
Milly saw, on the furthermost part of the lawn
A perfectly formed fairy ring.
A circle of toadstools that peeped through the grass
As if they'd been purposely planted
And Millicent knew if she stood in the ring
Any wish that she made would be granted.

So, closing her eyes as she stood in the ring
And crossing her fingers as well,
She begged any fairy who might be close by
To weave her a small magic spell.
'I don't want too much,' Milly whispered aloud,
'But I'm wishing as hard as can be,
If something goes wrong and annoys Mr Price
Please fairies, don't let it be me.'

Before they set off on the walk the next day
Mr Price scowled grimly at Milly
And rumbled, 'Now Millicent, stay close to me
And please – don't do anything silly.'
Millicent made a rude face at his back
Which I know you may think isn't nice
But one can forgive such a small lapse as that
Especially with teachers like Price.

226

The class wandered off through the woods by the
   church
Inspecting each new plant and flower.
Milly's wish had been granted, for all had gone well
And the class had been out for an hour,
So Milly confided in Angela Brown
She was under the fairies' protection
And Oliver Price, who had heard the remark,
Wandered in Milly's direction.

'Dear child,' he remarked in a sarcastic tone,
'Kindly address your attention
To matters in hand and of fairies and such
I prefer to hear no further mention.'
With that he reached out for a wild primrose flower
As if to examine the petals
And then, quite surprisingly, stumbled headfirst
Into a large clump of nettles.

It was all that the children could do not to laugh
As Mr Price rose looking flustered
And trying to conceal just how foolish he felt
He angrily bellowed and blustered.
Urging the children to hurry along
And threatening to punish their laughter
He strode down the path, still muttering with rage,
As the tittering children ran after.

They came to a stream and a small wooden bridge,
Mr Price made the children go first
Then made to cross over but slipped and fell in –
It seemed like the poor man was cursed.
For each time he tried to get out up the bank
He seemed to meet some strange resistance
And kept falling back, despite half the class
Rushing to give their assistance.

The class were in raptures and laughed till they cried
As back to the school they all straggled
With Oliver Price squelching slowly behind
Looking livid and sorely bedraggled.
He felt like a fool and he looked one as well
As he stood in the staffroom – still draining,
Soaking the carpet to such an extent
That the headmaster started complaining.

Millicent Mary and all of the class
Could hardly believe what they'd seen.
It was almost as if some invisible force
Had pushed Mr Price in the steam.
So take my advice, don't scoff at this tale,
An experience like Millicent Mary's
Might happen to you and it's safer by far
To believe there are such things as fairies.

Doug Millband

My Picture

My flame-picture painting
is pinned on the wall
and teacher says
it's a rainbow ball.

But though I'm pleased
I sometimes frown –
Dare I tell her today
it's upside down?

Archie Barrett

Art

Art is messy,
Paint everywhere.
Paint on the tables,
Paint on the chairs.
Paint on the desk lids,
Paint on the door.
Paint on the ceiling,
Paint on the floor.
Everyone likes Art,
What a merry caper;
There's paint all around the room,
But none on the paper!

Olivia Frances Hum (aged 9)

How to Paint the Portrait of a Bird

First paint a cage
with an open door
then paint
something pretty
something simple
something fine
something useful
for the bird
next place the canvas against a tree
in a garden
in a wood
or in a forest
hide behind the tree
without speaking
without moving . . .
Sometimes the bird comes quickly
but it can also take many years
before making up its mind
Don't be discouraged
wait
wait if necessary for years
the quickness or the slowness of the coming
of the bird having no relation
to the success of the picture
When the bird comes
if it comes
observe the deepest silence
wait for the bird to enter the cage
and when it has entered
gently close the door with the paint–brush
then
one by one paint out all the bars
taking care not to touch one feather of the bird

230

Next make a portrait of the tree
choosing the finest of its branches
for the bird
paint also the green leaves and the freshness of the
    wind
dust in the sun
and the sound of the insects in the summer grass
and wait for the bird to decide to sing
If the bird does not sing
it is a bad sign
a sign that the picture is bad
but if it sings it is a good sign
a sign that you are ready to sign
so then you pluck very gently
one of the quills of the bird
and you write your name in a corner of the picture.

Jacques Prévert,
(translated from the French by Paul Dehn)

Singing

The children are singing,
their mouths open like sleepy fish.
Our teacher conducting the class
waves her arms
like a rhyme in water.
The girls sing high:
our ears ring for the sweetness.
Listeners stand in dazzling amazement.

Peter Sheton (aged 10)

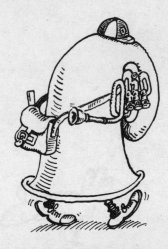

The High School Band

On warm days in September the high school band
Is up with the birds and marches along our street,
Boom boom,
To a field where it goes boom boom until eight
    forty-five
When it marches, as in the old rhyme, back, boom
    boom,
To its study halls, leaving our street
Empty except for the leaves that descend, to no
    drum,
And lie still.
In September
A great many high school bands beat a great many
    drums,
And the silences after their partings are very deep.

Reed Whittemore

Keeping the Score

They're going in to bat: Number One, Number
   Two . . .
It's a long walk to the wicket.
I wonder if he knows his pads are on the wrong
way round?
Where's my pencil? Anybody seen my pencil?
I've got to have one, I'm scoring . . .

Two runs.
No ball.

Two runs, no ball, one run. Two runs, no ball,
one run . . . Where *is* that pencil?
He's out! Can I borrow a pencil? Thank you, sir,
yes, sir; I'll give it back afterwards.
Two runs, no ball, one run . . . out.

It's a very long walk to the wicket.
Even longer back.
The sun's hot.
Bet it's hot out there.

Why are umpires always fat?

Now the point's broken! Why does it always
   happen to me?
Howzat!
Wait, my pencil's broken!
Sir, can I have another pencil? No, sir, I didn't
do it deliberately, sir, it just went . . .

Maiden over. That's an 'M', I think.

I wonder how high that cloud is?

Another maiden.

Wish I could sit under the trees. It's hot.

The fat umpire's got his coat on and two sweaters
round his neck. Why doesn't *he* get hot?

One run.

I wonder if anyone would mind if I went and scored
under the trees?

This pencil's too thick. What'll I do if it breaks?
I can't ask Sir again.

Howzat! Not out.

One day I'll fly a plane like that: so high up all
you can see is its trail.

I wonder where it's going.

Out!

Who's number four?

Come on, number four, where are you?

Crikey, it's me!

Score! Somebody score!

Who cares about the pencil . . . where's my bat?

Christopher Mann

Friday Morning Last Two Lessons is Games Day

We straggle in two's
Down Enbutt Lane to the playing fields
In a gap-toothed murmuring line
Filling the pavement.
Mr Pearson strides out in front
The ball tucked firmly under one arm,
His head bent.

We avoid lampposts
And young mothers pushing prams,
Sometimes walk gammy-legged in gutters
Or scuffle through damp leaves.
The morning is filled
With laughter-tongued and pottering mongrels;
Old men tending bare borders
Slowly unbend
And lean upon their brooms to watch us pass.
Their wives in flowered pinnies
Peer through the lace curtains
Of unused front rooms.

At the pitch
We change in the old pavilion
That smells of dust and feet
And has knot holes in the boarding.
Someone
From another class
Has left
One
Blue and white sock behind.

The lads shout about other games
And goals and saves and shots
Or row about who'll wear red or blue
Pearson blows exasperation
'Come on, lads, let's be having you

With eighteen a side
We tear after the ball shouting,
Longing to give it a good clean belt,
Perform some piece of perfection –
Beat three sprawling backs in a mazy dribble,
Race full pelt on to a plate-laid-on pass
And crack it full of hate and zest
Past the diving goalie to bulge the net.
But there is no net
And we have to leg it after the ball
To the allotments by the lane
Before we can take centre
To start the game again.

Afterwards,
Still wearing football socks,
Studded boots slung on my shoulder,
I say 'Tarrah' to Trev
At Station Road and drift home
Playing the game again.
Smoke climbs up from the neat red chimneys;
Babies drool and doze
And laugh at the empty sky.
There is the savour of cabbage and gravy
About the Estate and the flowers do not hear
The great crowd roaring me on.

Gareth Owen

Winter Sports

It's freezing outside and there's snow on the
 ground,
But the games master's leaping and dancing around.
He thinks that it's fun to be frozen and blue
And he wants to play football, so what can we do?
IS HE MAD?? Is he drunk? Has he got a screw
 loose?
We search high and low to find some excuse.

But alas none appears. To the pitches we jog,
And begin to play football. Not easy in fog.
Knees knock together, fingers turn blue,
The games master's yelling, he's passing to you,
'Run with the ball, boy, dribble and score,'
But there's snow in your boots and you can't take
 much more.

We've tried to play football, we've all done our best,
Now send for the husky dogs, skis and the rest.
Still the games master says that we've not had
 enough,
'You'll stay so that people can see that you're
 tough.'
But there'll be some surprise when they see through
 the mist
Twenty–two little snowmen and one waving his
 fist.

Charles Davies

A Wet Football Game

Wet and muddy, soaked right through,
  Covered with bruises, black, red and blue.
Socks at ankles, laces flying,
  I really almost feel like crying.
But wait a minute, did we win?
  How many goals did we get in?
More or less than the opposition?
  I can't remember my position.
Was I in goal or was I attack?
  I remember now – I was Left Back
Yes, we won by eight to two
  I'm glad my first football game is through!

Anon

Kevin Scores!

Kevin flicks the ball sideways, leaning
From it, letting it roll
Away, smoothly. He knows Tom is sprinting
Up from defence for it, down
The touchline, so he moves seriously beyond
The centre-half, hoping the ball will come
Over, perfectly, within the reach
Of his timed leap, so he can dive upward,
Feet pointed, arms balancing,
Arched like a hawk for the stab of his head at the
    goal.

He has seen it often, Law,
And Osgood on the telly,
How they wait hungrily
Under the ball floating over,
Then the great poise of the leap,
Almost too late you'd think,
Like great cats hunting,
Or sleek, muscular sharks,
Leaping beyond gravity, up, up,
Then the sharp snap of the head
And the white ball coldly in the net.

Kevin waits by the far post, willing
Tom to get the ball over.
He feels slack and alone, he can see
David in goal, elbows tensely bent, fingers
Stretched for catching in his old woollen gloves.
Tom sways inside the back, he takes
Two short steps, he swings
His left foot, and the ball lifts
Perfectly, perfectly,
Within the bound of Kevin's timed leap.
He is drawn to it, he straightens
In a slow upward dive, and he bends back,
Eyes rapt on the crossed ball he rises
To meet, and now
The sharp snap of his head
And the white ball coldly past the plunging David.

As he runs downfield he knows his face is laughing.

Leslie Norris

Jolly Hockey Sticks!

Elaine and I would crouch at the back.
If picked for the team our nerve would crack.
'Elaine, centre back. Teresa, left wing.
Get on your feet and give it some zing.'

Bully off, bully off! Why am I here?
Crikey! The ball's getting horribly near.
Brenda Stokes is waving her stick.
If she gets any closer I'll give her a kick.

I can't take any more of this grizzly game.
It's enough to make you wish you were lame.
What heavenly music! The whistle's blowing.
And that's the end of this pitiful poem.

Louise Draycott

Homework

'I'm not going to do my homework!'
I said, yesterday, with glee,
Boasting to friends as we made our way home.
'Why don't *you* skip it, like me?'

'I don't want to do my homework!'
Mother ignored my plea:
'Hurry up and finish eating,
Do your homework after tea.'

I can't concentrate on homework
With the family watching TV.
I pretended I had finished.
Mother didn't ask to see.

How I wished I had done my homework
As friends showed their books to me.
I *knew* I'd get into trouble –
Blank pages where my work should be!

Tonight I *will* do my homework.
Teachers always win, you see.
They made me miss swimming to complete it.
Tonight I'll do it *before* tea.

Marian Gosling

I Love to do my Homework

I love to do my homework.
It makes me feel so good.
I love to do exactly
As my teacher says I should.

I love to do my homework,
I never miss a day.
I even love the men in white
Who are taking me away.

Anon

The Last Exam
A villanelle

*A villanelle was a round song sung by French farmers in
the Middle Ages.*

To read the questions carefully
I hold my breath like a balloon.
After this one I'll be free

of European History,
of desks and people in this room,
after this one I'll be free.

'In the thirteenth century . . .'
It's much too hot this afternoon
to read the questions carefully.

I watch them scribble busily
as if there were no flaming June . . .
after this one I'll be free

to fish and swim down by the sea,
to lie and dream or watch the moon.
To read the questions carefully,

and answer them, I have to be
a wingless bug in a cocoon.
After this one I'll be free

to fly and make some history.
So I begin, in silent gloom,
to read the questions carefully.
After this one I'll be free.

Jane Whittle

Bad Report – Good Manners

My daddy said, 'My son, my son,
This school report is bad.'
I said, 'I did my best I did,
My dad my dad my dad.'
'Explain, my son, my son,' he said,
'Why *bottom* of the class?'
'I stood aside, my dad my dad,
To let the others pass.'

Spike Milligan

School Report

'TOO EASILY SATISFIED. SPELLING STILL
   POOR.
HER GRAMMAR'S ERRATIC. LACKS CARE.
WOULD SUCCEED IF SHE WORKED.
   INCLINED TO BE SMUG.'
I think that's a wee bit unfare.

Ah well, their it is! Disappointing perhaps,
For a mum what has always had brane,
But we can't all have looks or be good at our
   books . . .
She's her father all over agane.

Carole Paine

IN THE PLAYGROUND

Morning break

Andrew Flag plays football
Jane swings from the bars
Chucker Peach climbs drainpipes
Spike is seeing stars

Little Paul's a Martian
Anne walks on her toes
Ian Dump fights Kenny
Russell picks his nose

Dopey Di does hop-scotch
Curly drives a train
Maddox-Brown and Thompson
Stuff shoes down the drain

Lisa Thin throws netballs
Mitchell stands and stares
Nuttall from the first year
Shouts and spits and swears

Dick Fish fires his ray gun
Gaz has stamps to swop
Dave and Dan are robbers
Teacher is the cop

Betty Blob pulls faces
Basher falls . . . and dies
Tracey shows her knickers
Loony swallows flies

Faye sits in a puddle
Trev is eating mud
Skinhead has a nose bleed
– pints and pints of blood

Robbo Lump pings marbles
Murray hands out cake
What a lot of nonsense
During
   Morning
     Break

Wes Magee

In the Playground

In the playground
Some run round
Chasing a ball
Or chasing each other;
Some pretend to be
Someone on TV;
Some walk
And talk,
Some stand
On their hands
Against the wall
And some do nothing at all.

Stanley Cook

Complaint

The teachers all sit in the staffroom.
The teachers all drink tea.
The teachers all smoke cigarettes
As cosy as can be.

We have to go out at playtime
Unless we bring a note
Or it's tipping down with rain
Or we haven't got a coat.

We have to go out at playtime
Whether we like it or not.
And freeze to death if it's freezing
And boil to death if it's hot.

The teachers can sit in the staffroom
And have a cosy chat.
We have to go out at playtime;
Where's the fairness in that?

Allan Ahlberg

Skipping Songs

The High Skip,
The Sly Skip,
The Skip like a Feather,
The Long Skip,
The Strong Skip,
And the Skip All Together.

The Slow Skip,
The Toe Skip,
The Skip Double-Double
The Fast Skip,
The Last Skip,
And the Skip Against Trouble.

    One I love, two I loathe,
    Three I cast away;
    Four I love with all my heart,
    Five I love, I *say*.
    Six he loves me, seven he don't,
    Eight he'll marry me, nine he won't,
    Ten he would if he could, but he can't,
    Eleven he comes, twelve he tarries,
    Thirteen he's waiting, fourteen he marries.

    I took my girl to a ball one night
    And sat her down to supper,
    The table fell and she fell too,
    And stuck her nose in the butter.

Traditional

Skipping Song

Anne and Belinda
Turning the rope,
Helen jumps in
But she hasn't got a hope.
Helen Freckles
What will you do
Skip on the table
In the Irish Stew.
Freckles on her face
Freckles on her nose
Freckles on her knee caps
Freckles on her toes.

Helen Freckles
Tell me true
How many freckles have you got on you?
One, two, three, four, five, six . . .
And out goes you.

Stella Starwars
Skip in soon
In your spaceship
And off to the moon.
Skip on the pavement
One and two
Skip like a rabbit
Or a kangaroo;
Skip so high
You'll never come down;
Over the steeple
Over the town.
Skip over roof tops
Skip over trees
Skip over rivers
Skip over seas,
Skip over London
Skip over Rome
Skip all night
And never come home.
Skip over moonbeams
Skip over Mars
Skip through the Milky Way
And try to count the stars.
One, two, three, four, five, six . . .
And out goes you.

Gareth Owen
(from 'Skipping Song')

Counting-out Rhymes

Inty, tinty, tethery, methery,
Bank for over, Dover, ding,
Aut, taut, toosh;
Up the Causey, down the Cross,
There stands a bonnie white horse:
It can gallop, it can trot,
It can carry the mustard pot.
One, two, three, out goes she!

One-ery, two-ery, dickery, dee.
Halibo, crickbo, dandilee;
Pin, pan, myskee dan,
Tweddledum, twaddledum, twenty-one;
Black fish, white trout.
Eeny, meeny, you go out.

Hoky poky, winky wum,
How do you like your 'taters done?
Snip, snap, snorum,
High popolorum,
Kate go scratch it,
You are out.

Icker-backer
Soda-cracker
Icker-backer-boo
En-gine
Number nine
Out go you.

Traditional

254

Counting-out Rhyme

Silver bark of beech, and sallow
Bark of yellow birch and yellow
　　Twig of willow.

Stripe of green in moosewood maple,
Colour seen in leaf of apple,
　　Bark of popple.

Wood of popple pale as moonbeam,
Wood of oak for yoke and barn-beam,
　　Wood of hornbeam.

Silver bark of beech, and hollow
Stem of elder, tall and yellow
　　Twig of willow.

Edna St Vincent Millay

The Blue Ball

With many a bump
On the bouncy ground
Quiet and gentle
We pass it round;
Till Jennifer stumbles,
Sally-Ann fumbles,
And look, it's over
The playground wall!
PLEASE-WILL-YOU-THROW-US-BACK-
　　OUR-BALL?

Back now it comes.
Jimbo catches it
And holds it fast
Till Martin snatches it;
He throws to Tom,
Who, all unready,
Lets it go by;
It's caught by Teddy.
Teddy will keep it
As long as he can –
Toss it and bounce it;
But quickly Ann
Cries, 'Drop it you silly!'
In rushes Billy
And *kicks* it over
The playground wall!
PLEASE-WILL-YOU-THROW-US-BACK-
    OUR-BALL?

But close and sly
By the playground gate,
Big Bill Craddock
He lies in wait.
Straight to his feet
The blue ball bounces;
Bill Craddock leaps on it,
Bill Craddock pounces.
Look! Off he goes with it –
Cutting mad capers,
Does all he knows with it
Wild to escape us;
Turns a fierce grin
To the tongues that would scold him;
Tears himself free
From the hands that would hold him;

Uses his cunning
At tripping and running,
Turns about twistily,
Fights with his fist till he
Holds the ball high
And with a great cry
He *hurls* it over
The playground wall!
PLEASE-WILL-YOU-THROW-US-BACK-
 OUR-BALL?

John Walsh

Ball Bouncing Rhymes

Queen Caroline

Queen, Queen Caroline,
Dipped her hair in turpentine;
Turpentine made it shine,
Queen, Queen Caroline.

Through the Teeth

Through the teeth
And past the gums
Look out stomach,
Here it comes!

Order in the Court

Order in the court
The judge is eating beans
His wife is in the bath tub
Shooting submarines

Traditional

Whip Top

Whip top! Whip top!
Turn about and never stop!
Monday's top will spin away,
Tuesday's top will sing all day,
Wednesday's top is never slow,
Thursday's top to sleep will go,
Friday's top will dance about,
Saturday's top will tire you out!
Whip top! Whip top!
Spin around and never stop!

Anon

Conkers

When chestnuts are hanging
Above the school yard,
They are little green sea–mines
Spiky and hard.

But when they fall bursting
And all the boys race,
Each shines like a jewel
In a satin case.

Clive Sansom

Down in the Meadow

Down in the meadow
Where the green grass grows,
To see Sally Waters
Bloom like a rose:
Sally made a pudding,
She made it so sweet,
And never stuck a knife in
Till Johnny came to eat.
Taste love, taste love,
And don't say nay,
For next Monday morning
Is your wedding day.
He bought her a gown
And a guinea-gold ring,
And a fine cocked hat
To be married in.

Northampton playground game

The Alley–Alley–O

The big ship sails through the Alley–Alley–O
 the Alley–Alley–O, Alley–Alley–O,
The ship sails through the Alley–Alley–O
 on the last day of December!

Traditional

School

Bang! Slap! Punch!
Those two are having a fight.
One of them swings a nice left hook
The other swings a right.
The teacher comes to stop the fight –
And accidentally takes the right.

Patrick McCoy

Back in the Playground Blues

Dreamed I was in a school playground, I was about
  four feet high
Yes dreamed I was back in the playground and
  standing about four feet high
The playground was three miles long and the
  playground was five miles wide

It was broken black tarmac with a high fence all
  around
Broken black dusty tarmac with a high fence
  running all around
And it had a special name to it, they called it The
  Killing Ground.

Got a mother and a father, they're a thousand miles
  away
The Rulers of the Killing Ground are coming out to
  play
Everyone thinking: who they going to play with
  today?

    You get it for being Jewish
    Get it for being black
    Get it for being chicken
    Get it for fighting back
    You get it for being big and fat
    Get it for being small
    O those who get it get it and get it
    For any damn thing at all

Sometimes they take a beetle, tear off its six legs one by one
Beetle on its black back rocking in the lunchtime sun
But a beetle can't beg for mercy, a beetle's not half the fun

Heard a deep voice talking, it had that iceberg sound;
'It prepares them for Life' – but I have never found
Any place in my life that's worse than The Killing Ground.

Adrian Mitchell

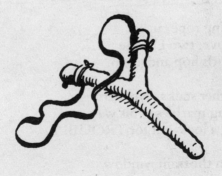

Winter Playground

In the cold winter sunshine
The children stand against the wall.
They look like washing on a line,

Neat red coat, stripey mitts,
Narrow green tights with a hole in the knee.
Still and stiff, frozen in a row.

Across the playground
Three boys are chasing a ball.
A little dog barks through the fence.

A skipping rope curves –
'One I love, two I loathe . . .'
As the girls hop and jump.

The teacher stalks, eyes darting,
Scattering marbles in his way,
Keeping a look-out for TROUBLE.

But from the train window
It's the still ones I see, the quiet ones,
Straight and stiff against the wall,
Like washing, frozen on the line.

Jenny Craig

SCHOOL FOOD

Whole Duty of Children

A child should always say what's true,
And speak when he is spoken to
And behave mannerly at table:
At least as far as he is able.

Robert Louis Stevenson

Come to the Cook-house Door

Come to the cook-house door,
Come to the cook-house door,
Fill your belly full of jelly,
Come to the cook-house door.

Traditional

Martha Munch

Martha Munch, Martha Munch,
Why can't you wait like the rest until lunch?
You've nibbled in Needlework,
Guzzled in Games,
Slurped through the Scripture class,
Called us all names.
Are you really so shocked when you see our surprise
As you greedily chew through a batch of pork pies?

Martha Munch, Martha Munch,
Eating bananas by wolfing the bunch.
You ate figs in the first lesson,
Steak in the second,
How much in the third lesson?
No one has reckoned.
The teachers are helpless, we all turn away,
You eat more in one lesson than we do all day.

Martha Munch, Martha Munch,
Why aren't you moving, the bell's gone for lunch?
Martha's trying to say something, trying to speak
But the food in her mouth makes her voice
    somewhat weak.
Then we realize with glee just how much we're in
    luck
Because Martha has eaten so much that she's stuck.
Trapped at her desk we can leave Martha Munch,
Today for us all there'll be plenty of lunch.

Charles Davies

Dinner Queue Dilemma

The boy stood in the dinner queue
And heaved a great big sigh.
He wondered what to eat today –
Egg and ham? Or pie?
Curry and rice? Or toad–in–the–hole?
Dumpling stew? Or fry?
Chips and beans? *No* horrid greens!
Whatever should he try?

At last he managed to reach the front,
And opened his mouth to speak . . .
'Everything's *off*,' the lady said,
'Except for bubble-and-squeak.'

Timothy Hattersley

School Dinners

If you stay to school dinners
Better throw them aside.
A lot of kids didn't,
A lot of kids died.
The meat is of iron,
The puds are of steel.
If the gravy don't get you,
The custard will.

Traditional

James Bond comes to Lunch

The day James Bond came to lunch at our school
He
Dive bomb'd a sausage
Kung Fu'd a carrot
Machine gunn'd a fish–cake
Swam through the custard
And
Kissed Agnes the dinner lady.

Tom Edwards

School Gravy

'Why don't you *eat*?' the mother said,
'Roast, veg, and Yorkshire pud,
You surely have an appetite?
You can't resist such food!'

A tear slipped down the small boy's face,
He sighed, and shook his head.
'Oh why can't you make gravy
Like they do at school?' he said.

The mother's face went scarlet.
'Mine is beyond compare!
It's meaty, juicy, tasty too,
With flavour rich and rare.'

The small boy nodded sadly.
'I know. I must agree.
But at school it's something *special*.
I . . . like the lumps, you see!'

Jenny Craig

Drinking Fountain

When I climb up
   To get a drink,
It doesn't work
   The way you'd think.

I turn it up.
   The water goes
And hits me right
   Upon the nose.

I turn it down
   To make it small
And don't get any
   Drink at all.

Marchette Chute

Pancake Day

Pancake day is a very happy day,
If we don't have a holiday we'll all run away,
Where shall we run, up High Lane,
And here comes the teacher with a great big cane.

Traditional

A Peanut sat on the Railroad Track

A peanut sat on the railroad track,
His heart was all a-flutter;
Along came a train – the 9.15 –
Toot, toot, peanut butter!

Anon

I Eat My Peas With Honey

I eat my peas with honey.
I've done it all my life.
It makes the peas taste funny
But it keeps 'em on the knife!

Anon

SCHOOL TEACHERS

Distracted the Mother said to her Boy

Distracted the mother said to her boy
'Do you try to upset and perplex and annoy?
Now, give me four reasons – and don't play the
    fool –
Why you shouldn't get up and get ready for school.'

Her son replied slowly, 'Well, mother, you see,
I can't stand the teachers and they detest me;
And there isn't a boy or a girl in the place
That I like or, in turn, that delights in my face.'

'And I'll give you two reasons,' she said, 'why you
    ought
Get yourself off to school before you get caught;
Because, first, you are forty and, next, you young
    fool,
It's your job to be there.
You're the head of the school.'

Gregory Harrison

New Teachers

New teachers
remind me of woodworm,
Just moved into
a new piece of wood.

Anon

Teachers

Teachers get stuck with the subjects they teach.
FRENCH wears wool cardigans, HISTORY's
  hair's bleached.

PHYSICS is fat and LATIN goes bald,
R.E. gets flat feet, COOKING cat–calls.

GEOGRAPHY always wears sweaters and jeans,
ART leather jackets with gaps in the seams.

ENGLISH has thick specs and spots and a grin,
CHEMISTRY laughs a lot, MUSIC is thin.

MATHS has a habit of biting his nails,
DRAMA has big eyes and goes off to Wales.

BIOLOGY runs about puffing and shouting,
P.E.'s in the pub on every school outing.

Subjects get stuck to the people who teach them.
The people I like do the subjects I'm keen on.

Jane Whittle

He Who owns the Whistle rules the World

January wind and the sun
playing truant again.
Rain beginning to scratch
its fingernails across
the blackboard sky

in the playground
kids divebomb, corner
at silverstone or execute
traitors. Armed
with my Acme Thunderer
I step outside,
take a deep breath
and bring the world
to a standstill

Roger McGough

Words with Teacher

These are the words that teachers use:
Hypothesis, hypotenuse,
Isosceles, trapezium,
Potassium, magnesium,
Denominator, catechism
And antidisestablishmentarianism.

Colin West

A Close Shave

Another day is on the way
As the pips start ringing in my ear

Oh no! I forgot my letter about the other day
When I was away. Trouble!

She comes walking in the door
She gets closer to the drawer
She gets the register out
She starts to call the names
She gets closer and closer to my name
I'm going to be in trouble
I say yes!
She goes on!
She forgot, forgot, FORGOT!

David Bryant

A Teacher

A teacher's got a temper
like a bull.
He growls and roars
like a tiger,
he stamps and gets mad
and sometimes he's glad
he did it.

Bruce McGregor (aged 11)

A Schoolmaster's Admonition

Good children, refuse not these lessons to learn,
The pathway to virtue you here may discern;
In keeping them truly you shall be most sure
The praise of all people thereby to procure.

Be comely and decent in all thy array,
Not wantonly given to sport and to play;
But labour by virtue, in youth, to obtain
The love of thy betters, their friendship to gain.

The morning appearing, rise thou with speed,
Wash hands and face cleanly before thou go feed;
Let shoes be fast tied both, close to thy feet,
The better to travel all day in the street.

If thou be a scholar, to school make good haste,
For he is a truant that cometh there last;
For if thou dost loiter and play by the way,
Be sure with thy master it will cause a fray.

Swear not, nor curse not; delight not to steal;
Thy master obey thou; his secrets conceal;
Take heed of false lying; set no man at strife;
Nor be thou too desperate to strike with a knife.

And now, to conclude, bear this well in mind,
A diligent scholar much favour shall find;
But such as will loiter, and lazy will be,
Shall for their labour be brought on their knee.

Anon (1625)

Writing Right

Said a boy to his teacher one day,
'Wright has not written 'rite' right, I say!'
And the teacher replied
As the error she eyed:
'Right! – Wright, write 'rite' right, right away!'

Anon

If the Teacher was a Robot

If the teacher was a robot,
Made of Iron and Tin
We could take it all to pieces
And put it in the bin.
We'd loosen all its nuts and bolts
In the metalwork room,
We would weld its mouth tight shut,
And send it to its doom.

Paul Marsh (aged 13)

A Teacher from Harrow

There was a young teacher from Harrow
Whose nose was too long and too narrow.
It gave so much trouble
That he bent it up double
And wheeled it round school in a barrow.

Anon

A Teacher from Leeds

There once was a teacher from Leeds
Who swallowed a packet of seeds.
In less than an hour
Her nose was a flower
And her hair was a posy of weeds.

Anon

Thoughts

All people that on Earth do dwell,
Hope Mr Foster isn't in a bad mood,
Wonder if he's here yet?
Bet he's having his breakfast,
Come ye before him and rejoice.

The piano's wobbly,
Might fall over,
Without our aid he did us make,
Hope Mr Foster's ill,
And for his sheep he doth us take,

O enter then his gates with praise,
Latin room's empty,
Approach with joy his courts unto,
I'm in detention today,
Have to write out 100 lines,
For it is seemly so to do.

Marcus Holburn (aged 10)

Daydreams

Miss Barter thinks I'm reading,
But I'm taming lions,
or stalking kangaroos . . .
I am on the moon . . .
or swimming under water.
I have a fight with an octopus
and a giant sword fish . . .
I go home late at night
with ten fish
I caught in the river.

Miss Barter thinks I'm listening –
But no.
I'm boxing for the navy . . .
I'm diving off a cliff,
or throwing custard pies
at the circus.
I am a strong man,
big and lumpy . . .
I sit and float
in a big balloon
soaring through the clouds,
floating swiftly.

I think of racing a big train
in a sports car,
the wind rushing by:
I go round a bend
and go through a duck pond! . . .
When I wake up
I'm all blue –
The ink has gone over.

Richard Compton, (aged 10)

Miss Norma Jean Pugh,
First Grade Teacher

Full of oatmeal
And gluggy with milk
On a morning in spring time
Soft as silk
When legs feel slow
And bumble bees buzz
And your nose tickles from
Dandelion fuzz
And you long to
Break a few
Cobwebs stuck with
Diamond dew
Stretched right out
In front of you –
When all you want
To do is *feel*
Until it's time for
Another meal,
Or sit right down
In the cool
Green grass
And watch the
Caterpillars pass . . .
Who cares if
Two and two
Are four or five
Or red or blue?

Who cares whether
Six or seven
Come before or after
Ten or eleven?
Who cares if
C – A – T
Spells cat or rat
Or tit or tat
Or ball or bat?
Well, I do
But I didn't
Used to –
Until MISS NORMA JEAN PUGH!
She's terribly old
As people go
Twenty-one-or-five-or-six
Or so
But she makes a person want to
KNOW!

Mary O'Neill

I was Mucking About in Class

I was mucking about in class

Mr Brown said,
Get out and take your chair with me
I suppose he *meant* to say
Take your chair with you
so Dave said,
Yeah – you heard what he said
           get out and take my chair with him
so Ken said,
Yeah – get out and take his chair with me
so I said to Mr Brown
Yessir – shall I take our chair with you, sir?

Wow
that meant BIG TROUBLE

Michael Rosen

SCHOOL PETS AND OTHER
PEOPLE

Tashy the School's Rabbit

We clean his play pen
    every day
When we've finished we
    go out to play.
Miss Grundy gives him her
    home–made bread,
Tashy's pram is shining
    red.
Tashy sleeps in his wooden
    hutch
We all love him very
    much.
Tashy's eyes are very bright,
His furry coat is black
    and white.
He goes home with all
    his kind friends,
We wouldn't leave
    him in school at weekends.
Sometimes he's in a
    naughty mood,
But this doesn't put him
    off his food.
Tashy runs and scampers
    free,
When he's tired he sleeps
    on my knee.

If it is warm he goes out
    on the grass,
The children shout, 'Hello'
    as they pass
Carrots, oats and pears he
    loves to eat
He then runs round Miss
    Grundy's feet.
He begs, he searches, he
    jumps on our knees
Just 'cos he's looking
    for dandelion leaves.
At home–time it's into
    his pen and close the door
Tashy settles down and
    sleeps on his straw.

Rachel Teggert (aged 7)

The Goldfish

Jimmy Slater bullied me
And Brian Wilkins laughed at me
But when I was teased
Or lonely
Or sad
I would go to the prefab
Behind the bike sheds but
Before the gym
That housed the aquarium.

I would sit
Amid the flashing brilliance of the guppies
Under the wise watchful eyes of ancient terrapins
But I would watch the goldfish
Humble and beautiful
Simple and majestic
As it glided through its
Tangled weeds and greenish stones
As unaware as I was
Of the laughing eyes
Watching me
Watching the fish.

Until one day
Feeling low
I came to watch
But found instead
Smashed glass and
A trickle of water from
The bench to the floor.
And there,
Surrounded by the broken shards,
Limp weed trailing over its fin,
Lay the goldfish,
Dazzling in the harsh light.

Tom Edwards

Zebra Crossing

There is a Lollipopman
At the zebra crossing
With lollipops
He is trying
To lure zebras across
He makes me cross.
I cross.

Roger McGough

Lost

Dear Mrs Butler, this is just a note
About our Raymond's coat
Which he came home without last night,
So I thought I'd better write.

He was minus his scarf as well, I regret
To say; and his grandma is most upset
As she knitted it and it's pure
Wool. You'll appreciate her feelings, I'm sure.

Also, his swimming towel has gone
Out of his PE bag, he says, and one
Of his socks, too – it's purplish and green
With a darn in the heel. His sister Jean

Has a pair very similar. And while
I remember, is there news yet of those fairisle
Gloves which Raymond lost that time
After the visit to the pantomime?

Well, I think that's all. I will close now,
Best wishes, yours sincerely, Maureen Howe
(Mrs). PS I did once write before
About his father's hat that Raymond wore

In the school play and later could not find,
But got no reply. Still, never mind,
Raymond tells me now he might have lost the note,
Or left it in the pocket of his coat.

Allan Ahlberg

292

Mr Fitzsimmons

Mr Fitzsimmons,
Our caretaker, is tall
For reaching pictures
Down from the wall,
Looking over gates
And piled-up crates.
Just the height
To put new bulbs
In electric lights
Or discover
What was lost
On top of cupboards.
He has a key
Worn shiny in his pocket
For every door
And a polisher
Plugging in at the socket
For every floor.
He brushes school clean
And polishes it bright
Every night.

Stanley Cook

Mr Mole

The person I know best at school
stays out of sight as a rule
keeping warm in a dusty old room
with a bucket, a mop and a broom.

If it's too cold to shiver outside
he has let me join him inside
while he brews up his afternoon tea.
He once shared a sandwich with me.

Mr Mole lost a leg in The War
but the wooden one's more useful for
planting out lettuces, he says,
when he does his Allotment on Sundays.

His job is a School Janitor
but he works more at being a gardener,
growing onions, carrots and cabbages.
He refuses to say what his age is.

Mr Mole says the earth and the air
have made him a young millionaire.

Jane Whittle

The School Nurse

We're lining up to see the nurse
And in my opinion there's nothing worse.
It is the thing I always dread.
Supposing I've got *nits* in my head.

I go inside and sit on the chair.
She ruffles her fingers in my hair.
I feel my face getting hot and red.
Supposing she finds *nits* in my head.

It's taking ages; it must be bad.
Oh, how shall I tell my mum and dad?
I'd rather see the dentist instead
Than be the one with *nits* in his head.

Then she taps my arm and says, 'Next please!'
And I'm out in the corridor's cooling breeze.
Yet still I can feel that sense of dread.
Supposing she *had* found nits in my head.

Allan Ahlberg

After Adrian Mitchell – We Liked His Stuff!

You came up from London with it.
Came into our school with it.
POETRY
We liked your stuff!

You took all your books from it.
We got lots of laughs from it.
POEM BAG
We liked your stuff!

For your birthday you were given it.
Took it off when you got hot in it.
LEATHER JACKET
We liked your stuff!

Many a cat was killed by it.
Everyone was filled by it.
CURIOSITY
We liked your stuff!

All your poems are printed on it.
Some are still in scribbles on it.
PAPER
We liked your stuff!

You failed your exams for it.
Our mums and dads all danced to it.
ROCK AND ROLL
We liked your stuff!

Lines in your poems created it.
Children burst right out with it.
LAUGHTER
We liked your stuff!

Excitement in the classroom –
Ideas in our head –
Creating, thinking, writing –
We were the poets instead.
For you we created them.
Then we went away with them.
POEMS
Because we liked your stuff!

*Class 9, Tyldesly County
Primary School*

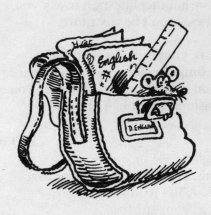

Intelligence Test

'What do you use your eyes for?'
The white–coated man enquired.
'I use my eyes for looking,'
Said Toby, – 'unless I'm tired.'

'I see. And then you close them,'
Observed the white–coated man.
'Well done. A very good answer.
Let's try another one.

What is your nose designed for?
What use is the thing to you?'
'I use my nose for smelling,'
Said Toby, 'Don't you, too?'

'I do indeed,' said the expert,
'That's what the thing is for.
Now I've another question to ask you,
Then there won't be any more.

'What are your ears intended for?
Those things at each side of your head?
Come on – don't be shy – I'm sure you can say.'
'For washing behind,' Toby said.

Vernon Scannell

Aristotle and Ballcocks

They sent me to see the careers man,
He was in a posh office down town,
I tried to be pleasant and friendly,
But all I received was a frown.

'I'm sorry to have to inform you,
But it takes more than three CSEs,
Especially as one is in woodwork,
And the others are only grade threes,

'It takes years of hard work to be one,
Philosophers aren't trained they are born,
And besides your "qualifications",
There isn't a box on the form.'

So he sent me away with a leaflet,
To get on a GYOS★
By the time I walked home from the bus stop,
I thought, 'Oh hell, what a mess!'

When I told my dad, he couldn't stop laughing,
His face went all purple and red,
And when he recovered from choking,
He told me, 'Try plumbing instead,'

So I looked it up on my leaflet,
And filled in the space on the form,
I read up on ballcocks and U-bends,
And reflected the fate of a pawn.

If Descartes had had this problem,
And Aristotle and Socrates too,
We might not have had great thinkers,
But just think of the showers and loos!

So I went back to see the careers man,
Who said, 'It's a safer idea,
To stick to something more normal,
A job and not a career.'

Emma Payne (aged 15)

*Government Youth Opportunity Scheme
as it was called when I wrote this.

GOING HOME

Three more days of school
Three more days of sorrow
Three more days of this old dump
And we'll be home tomorrow.

Traditional

There's a Ladybird on Carol's Hair

There's a ladybird on Carol's hair
My chair leg's on my shoe,
I've yawned four times while teacher reads.
Do you think this story's true?
A giant with a beard of grass?
A castle made of soap?
I'd like to roll our vicar down
The Quarry's muddy slope.
I'm nearly seven,
I'm nearly seven,
I'm glad I've got a mole;
Yes, silly, in the garden shed,
I've covered it with coal;
My bottom's aching,
Can't we go?
Yes, up and chairs on desks
And all our hands together, so,
And keep us safe till morning light.
My cousin's got a lovely kite.
Ho, ho; ho, ho.
Yes Miss. Good night.

G. Harrison
(from 'Ploughing after School')

The Last Lesson of the Afternoon

I sit here in slumber, hitting my head
and chewing my pencil.
The teacher is groaning.
The clock ticks like a nightmare.
My cartridge is dry except for a few splotches.
The room is bare like a prison cell.
My back is aching and my fingers are like
an alien's with blue ink.
I gaze up and only see whiteness.
My desk wobbles.
I listen,
all I can hear is pens writing.
The teacher's desk is a mountain of books.
Then I am saved, the school bell rings!
There is a mad scramble to escape.
I get outside – and feel a breeze
gently go by me.

Justin Bailey (aged 9)

Evening Schoolboys

Hearken to that happy shout – the schoolhouse door
Is open thrown, and out the youngsters teem;
Some run to leapfrog on the rushy moor,
And others dabble in the shallow stream,
Catching young fish and turning pebbles o'er
For mussel clams. Look in that mellow gleam
Where the retiring sun that rests the while
Streams through the broken hedge. How happy
   seem
Those schoolboy friendships leaning o'er the stile,
Both reading in one book; anon a dream
Rich with new joys doth their young hearts beguile,
And the book's pocketed most hastily.
Ah, happy boys, well may ye turn and smile,
When joys are yours that never cost a sigh.

John Clare

For a Junior School Poetry Book

The mothers are waiting in the yard.
Here come the children, fresh from school.
The mothers are wearing rumpled skirts.
What prim mouths, what wrinkly cheeks.
The children swirl through the air to them,
trailing satchels and a smell of chalk.

The children are waiting in the yard.
The mothers come stumbling out of school.
The children stare primly at them,
lace their shoes, pat their heads.
The mothers swirl through the air to cars.
The children crossly drive them home.

The mothers are coming.
The children are waiting.
The mothers had eyes that see
boiled eggs, wool, dung and bed.
The children have eyes that saw
owl and mountain and little mole.

Christopher Middleton

Oh, Joyous House

When I walk home from school,
I see many houses,
Many houses down many streets.
They are warm, comfortable houses,
But other people's houses.
I pass without much notice.

Then as I walk farther, farther
I see a house, the house.
It springs up with a jerk
That speeds my pace; I lurch forward.
Longing makes me happy, I bubble inside.
It's my house.

Richard Janzen (aged 12)

Walking Home

There are
523 railings
29 steps
7 bus stops
14 trees
32 houses
1 antique shop
25 drains
And 1 roundabout
Between my house and school.

Tom Edwards

School's Over

School's over.

'Bye Lizz!'
'Bye Mandy!'
'Bye!'
Sun shouts
Like enormous tubas.
Women with tousled hair
Loll in doorways,
Too hot to chatter.
Their babies cry
And they do not care.

Home at last.
The house is lonely.
Dad's on the buses.
Mum works at the Co–op.
Lonely is cool.
Lonely is quiet.
I like it.
I read a bit
Then flick over the pages of the book
Impatient to get to the end.
No pictures.
I draw my own.
The heroine has brown hair and freckles.
The villain's a greasy grey.
Those caves under the hill
Where he hides the treasure?

An hour has passed.
Lonely is empty.
Is big, bare spaces
I'm afraid to cross.
No cat to purr
And rub against my legs.
Mum hates them.
Dad says they smell
Like geranium leaves.
I walk from room to room
Looking for my cat,
My dusty gold cat
With gooseberry eyes.
'Puss! Puss!' I say,
'Here's a bowl of cream for you.'
But he never comes.

Olive Dove

Index of titles

Index of First Lines

316

Acknowledgements

The author and publishers would like to thank the following people for giving permission to include in this anthology material which is their copyright. The publishers have made every effort to trace copyright holders. If we have inadvertently omitted to acknowledge anyone we should be most grateful if this could be brought to our attention for correction at the first opportunity.

Karen Aldous and Lewknor School for 'The New Boy'.
Angus and Robertson (UK) Limited for 'The Porter' and 'The Barber' by C. J. Dennis from *A Book for Kids*.
Bogle L'Ouverture Publications Limited for 'Confusion' by Odette Thomas from *Rain Falling, Sun Shining*.
Jonathan Cape Limited on behalf of Roger McGough for 'First Day at School', 'A Good Poem', 'Streemin' and 'Nooligan' from *In the Classroom*; on behalf of the Executors of the W. H. Davies Estate for 'School's Out' from *Complete Poems*; and on behalf of Fay Maschler for 'The Bully' from *A Child's Book of Manners*.
Tony Connor for 'Child's Bouncing Song' from *Lodgers*, published by Oxford University Press.
Graeme Curry for 'The Pass', 'The Battle' and 'Jobs' by Benjamin Bolt.
The Literary Trustees of Walter de la Mare and The Society of Authors as their representative for 'The Dunce' by Walter de la Mare from *Peacock Pie*.
André Deutsch for 'I'm a Man' by Michael Rosen from *Mind Your Own Business* and 'Maths Problems' by Alvin Schwartz from *A Twister of Twists*.
Dennis Dobson Publishers for 'The ABC' by Spike Milligan from *The Little Pot Boiler*.
Mrs Gwen Dunn for 'I Went Back' and 'Saturdays' from *The Live-long Day*, published by BBC Radio for Schools.
The Feminist Press for 'Choosing Sides' by Siv Widerberg from *I'm Like Me*, translated by Verne Moberg, copyright © 1968, 1969, 1970, 1971 Siv Widerberg; translation copyright © 1973 Verne Moberg.
Roger Gibbs for 'Football Game' from *The Live-long Day*, published by BBC Radio for Schools.
Elizabeth M. Graham-Yooll for 'Morning Prayers'.
Hamish Hamilton Limited for 'Exercise Book' by Jacques Prévert, translated by Paul Dehn, from *The Fern on the Rock*, copyright © Dehn Enterprises Limited, 1965, 1976.

David Higham Associates for 'Timothy Winters' by Charles
Causley from *Collected Poems*, published by Macmillan; for 'School
Bell' by Eleanor Farjeon from *The Children's Bells*, published by
Oxford University Press; for 'Homework' by Russell Hoban from
Egg Thoughts; and for 'Children's Song' by Dylan Thomas from
Under Milk Wood, published by Dent.

Hodder & Stoughton Children's Books for 'Going to School in
the Country' and 'Going to School in the Town' by Leonard Clark
from *The Singing Time*.

Lutterworth Press for 'The English Language' by Harry Hemsley
from *Imagination*.

Brian Lee and Penguin Books Limited for 'Words' from *Late Home*.

John Murray (Publishers) Limited for 'Walking from School' from
Summoned by Bells by John Betjeman.

Gareth Owen and Penguin Books Limited for 'Our School',
'Winter', 'The Fight', 'Saturdays' and 'Sitting on Trev's back wall
on the last day of the holidays trying to think of something to do'
from *Salford Road*.

Oxford University Press for 'Out of School' from *Tomorrow is my
Love* by Hal Summers.

Lydia Pender for 'Marbles in my Pocket' from *Soundings* published
by Holmes McDougall Limited.

Daniel Pettiward for 'Top-secret School'.

The Poetry Society and Book Club Associates for 'Maths Lesson
Rules' by Christine Bates and Jill Etheridge; 'Poets' by Elaine
Breden; '11 Bus' by S. Hale; 'Board Rubber' by Gina Staley and
'The Toe Picker' by Debbie Ward, all from *Poets in School*.

Punch Publications Limited for 'Career' by Daniel Pettiward.

Michael Rosen and Penguin Books Limited for 'Rodge Said' and
'Here are the Football Results', part of 'You Tell Me' from *You Tell
Me* by Roger McGough and Michael Rosen.

R. C. Scriven for 'The Marrog' and 'Cricketer' from *The Live-long
Day* published by BBC Radio for Schools.

Robert Sparrow for 'Dinner Lady', 'Poor Simon Benn' and 'After
School'.

Studio Vista for 'From the classroom window' by Neil Bartlett and
'My Teacher' by Kevin Brown from *Poems for Children* edited by
Leonard Clark, published in 1970.

Phyllis Telfer for 'The School Bus Breaks Down' by Phyllis Telfer
and Hermea Goodman from *Chosen for Children*.

Shirley Toulson for 'Parents Evening' from *Allsorts 4*, published by
Macmillan Publishers Limited.

Mrs A. M. Walsh for 'From the Classroom Window' by John Walsh from *The Truants* published by William Heinemann Limited; and for 'I've Got an Apple Ready', 'Bus to School' and 'The Bully Asleep' by John Walsh from *The Roundabout by the Sea*, published by Oxford University Press.

Franklin Watts Limited for 'Banananananananana' and 'Good News' by William Cole from *A Boy Named Mary Jane*.

Jane Whittle for 'The Lollipop Lady', 'In Hall' and 'The Dinner Lady'.

Archie Barrett for 'My Picture'.

Bell & Hyman Publishers for 'Millicent and the Nature Ramble' by Doug Millband from *The Mishaps of Millicent Mary*.

Martin Brian & O'Keeffe Limited for 'The Magician' by Shaun Traynor from *Images of Winter*.

Cadbury Limited for 'Aristotle and Ballcocks' by Emma Payne, 'Go Away and Shut Up', by Colleen Boland, 'Thoughts' by Marcus Holburn and 'If the Teacher was a Robot' by Paul Marsh from *Cadbury's First Book of Children's Poetry*; 'Art' by Olivia Frances Hum, 'This 'Ere School' by Stephanie Marshall, 'First Day at School' by Melanie Louise Skipper and 'Tashy the School's Rabbit' by Rachel Teggert from *Cadbury's Second Book of Children's Poetry*; 'The Bully' by Paul Dingle, 'School' by Patrick McCoy, 'When I Was Lonely' by Teresa Steele, 'After Adrian Mitchell – We Liked His Stuff!' by Class 9, Tyldesly County Primary School from *Cadbury's Third Book of Children's Poetry*; and for 'I don't know' by Mhairi Boyle and 'Red Ink' by Sarah Rogers from Cadbury's 1986 Poetry Competition.

Jonathan Cape Limited on behalf of Roger McGough for 'He Who Owns the Whistle, Rules the World' from *In the Classroom*; on behalf of Adrian Mitchell for 'Dumb Insolence' from *The Apeman Cometh*.

Stanley Cook for 'The School', 'In the Playground' and 'Mr Fitzsimmons'.

Century Hutchinson for 'The Good, the Bored and the Ugly', and 'A Survey of Sovereigns' from *It's Funny When You Look At It* by Colin West; 'The Painful Way to Multiply', 'Words with Teacher' and 'Big Jim' from *Not To Be Taken Seriously* by Colin West; 'Back in the Playground Blues' by Adrian Mitchell from *I See a Voice* ed. Michael Joseph; and for 'Arithmetic' by Gavin Ewart from his *Collected Poems*. Marchette Chute for 'Drinking Fountain' from *Around and About* published by Dutton, 1957.

Charles Davies for 'The Old School Bus', 'Martha Munch' and 'Winter Sports'.

André Deutsch for 'Riddle' by John Cunliffe from *Riddles & Rhymes & Rigmaroles*.

Peter Dixon for 'Oh Bring Back Higher Standards'.

Dobson Books Ltd for 'First Primrose' by Leonard Clark from *Good Company*.

Olive Dove for 'School's Over' and 'Write a Poem'.

Louise Draycott for 'Jolly Hockey Sticks!'.

Tom Edwards for 'James Bond Comes to Lunch', 'The Goldfish' and 'Walking Home'.

The English Centre, London for 'Us Dreads' by Dave Martin, 'I am a Deemmun' by Julia Ignatiou and 'A Close Shave' by David Bryant, all from *City Lines*.

Gomer Press for 'Thug' by Raymond Garlick from *Incense*.

Marian Gosling for 'Homework'.

Hamlyn Publishing Group for 'The Bionic Boy' by Charles Connell from *Versicles and Limericks*.

Harper & Row Limited for 'Six Times One' by Karla Kuskin from *Near the Window Tree*.

Harrap Limited and Little, Brown and Company for 'Lmntl' by David McCord from *Mr Bidery's Spidery Garden*.

Gregory Harrison for 'Distracted the Mother said to her Boy' from *A Fourth Poetry Book*, compiled by John Foster, first published by Oxford University Press, 1982, and for 'There's a Ladybird on Carol's Hair', an extract from 'Ploughing After School', from *Posting Letters*, published by Oxford University Press.

Timothy Hattersley for 'Dinner Queue Dilemma'.

William Heinemann Limited and Doubleday for 'Miss Norma Jean Pugh, First Grade Teacher' by Mary O'Neill from *People I'd Like to Keep*.

David Higham Associates for 'The Fight' by Ted Walker, 'Conkers' by Clive Sansom, 'The Schoolboy' by Dylan Thomas and 'Summer Goes' by Russell Hoban.

Hodder & Stoughton Children's Books for 'First Day at School' and 'The Bully' by Rod Hull from *The Reluctant Poet*.

Julie Holder for 'The Loner'.

Paul Johnson for '1 × 1 is 2'.

Librairie Gallimard for 'How to Paint the Portrait of a Bird' by Jacques Prévert, translated by Paul Dehn, from *Paroles*.

Macdonald & Co. (Publishers) Limited for 'Lizzie' by Michael Rosen from *Wheel Around the World*.

Macmillan Publishing Company for 'The High School Band' by

Reed Whittemore from *The Self-Made Man and Other Poems*, ©
Reed Whittemore 1959.

Wes Magee for 'Morning Break'.

Christopher Mann for 'I Don't want to go to School Today', and
'Johnson Broke My Ruler, Sir'. 'Government Health Warning',
'Science' and 'Keeping the Score'.

Michael Joseph for 'Bad Report' by Spike Milligan from *Unspun
Socks From a Children's Laundry*.

Chirstopher Middleton for 'For a Junior School Poetry Book'.

Nerehurst Ltd for 'Red Cows' by Lydia Pender from *Poems for Fun*.

Leslie Norris for 'The Rebel Child' and 'Kevin Scores'.

Gareth Owen for 'A Stomach-ache is Worse Away from Home'
and 'Friday Morning Last Two Lessons is Games Day'.

Penguin Books Limited for 'Hullo, Inside' by Max Fatchen from
Wry Rhymes for Troublesome Times, Kestrel Books © Max Fatchen
1983; 'Complaint', 'Lost' and 'The School Nurse' by Allan Ahlberg
from *Please Mrs Butler*, Kestrel Books, © Allan Ahlberg, 1983.

A. D. Peters & Co. Limited for 'The Leader' and 'Zebra Crossing'
by Roger McGough from *Sky in the Pie*, Kestrel Books, 1983.

Punch for 'School Report' by Carole Paine.

Deborah Rogers Ltd for 'The Lesson' by Edward Lucie-Smith.

Michael Rosen for 'I was Mucking about in Class', first published
in *A Third Poetry Book*, compiled by John Foster, Oxford
University Press, 1982.

Vernon Scannell for 'Intelligence Test' from *The Apple Raid*.

Simon & Schuster, Inc. for 'The Wind' by James Snyder from
Miracles, © Richard Lewis 1966; 'Oh, Joyous House' by Richard
Janzen from *Miracles* © Richard Lewis 1966.

Stainer & Bell Limited for 'Impressions of a New Boy' by Marian
Collihole from *Themework*.

Shirley Toulson for 'The Changeling'.

Mrs A. M. Walsh for 'The Blue Ball' from *The Roundabout by the
Sea* by John Walsh (OUP).

Jane Whittle for 'Mr Mole', 'Teachers', 'The Last Exam',
'Thinking' and 'The Computer'.

Raymond Wilson for 'Playing Truant', first published in *A Fourth
Poetry Book*, compiled by John Foster, Oxford Univesity Press, 1982.

I REMEMBER, I REMEMBER

Famous People's Favourite
Childhood Poems

Compiled by ROB FARROW
Illustrated by TREVOR NEWTON

*D*ip into these memorable poems, picked by a
dazzling array of celebrities. Find out why
they've chosen each poem – or in Gazza's case,
how he became a poet for the day...

JUST ME by Paul Gascoigne

I'm a professional footballer
lying in a hospital bed
thinking of all those nasty things
all going through my head

I know I should not be lying here
it's because of Wembley
thinking of that stupid tackle...

Ooops! Sorry, you'll have to net a copy of the book if
you want to find out what happens next!

I REMEMBER, I REMEMBER
RED FOX paperback, £3.50 ISBN 0 09 931831 8

BUMWIGS and Earbeetles
and other Unspeakable Delights

Poems by ANN ZIETY
Illustrated by LESLEY BISSEKER

Think ghastly! Think grisly! Think grim! BUMWIGS AND EARBEETLES is all those things... and worse!!!

Smelly socks, crumbly compost heaps and mangy moggies are among the unthinkable, unspeakable delights in this collection.

Catch a whiff of this...

MY DOG NEVER HAD FLEAS

he had bumwigs and earbeetles
and sinus larvae
and one or two exaggerated boils
and bits of ticks that stuck to his ears
and sticky mites
and bites from fights
and stashes and stashes of nasty rashes
but he never had fleas
not one

RED FOX paperback, £3.50 ISBN 0 09 953961 6

BODLEY HEAD hardback, £8.99 ISBN 0 370 31975 3

A NOISY NOISE ANNOYS

Compiled by JENNIFER CURRY
Illustrated by SUSIE JENKIN-PEARCE

*B*ursting with poetic talent from Brian
Patten and William Shakespeare to
Thomas Hardy and Wes Magee, A NOISY
NOISE ANNOYS will take you on an aural
adventure of awesome proportions!
Sounds good? Great! Now read on...

No nerve was left unjangled
When Nicola learnt the fiddle.
She scraped it high
She scraped it low
She scraped it in the middle.

Mike Jubb

RED FOX paperback, £3.50 ISBN 0 09 952801 0
THE BODLEY HEAD hardback, £9.99 ISBN 0 370 32301 7

Colin Dann

THE CITY CATS SERIES

By the author of the award-winning
THE ANIMALS OF FARTHING WOOD

King of the Vagabonds
Sammy's survival instincts are put to the ultimate
test when he strays into the dangerous wilds of
Quartermile Field - where he is to be crowned...
King of the Vagabonds.
ISBN 0 09 921192 0 £3.50

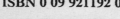

The City Cats
Sammy and Pinkie are enjoying their new life in the
big city. Pinkie's expecting kittens and proud Sammy
is top cat of the neighbourhood - but how long will
their good life last?
ISBN 0 09 921202 1 £3.50

And coming soon!

Copycat
When there's a purge on the stray cats and dogs in
the city of London, Sammy and Pinkie find
themselves in the middle of a life or death situation...
ISBN 0 09 21212 9

❖ Tales of Redwall ❖
BRIAN JACQUES

'Not since Roald Dahl have children filled their
shelves so compulsively' *The Times*

*An award-winning, best-selling series from
master storyteller, Brian Jacques.
Discover the epic* Tales of Redwall *adventures
about Redwall Abbey - and beyond!*

- **Martin the Warrior** 0 09 928171 6
- **Mossflower** 0 09 955400 3
- **Outcast of Redwall** 0 09 960091 9
- **Mariel of Redwall** 0 09 992960 0
- **The Bellmaker** 0 09 943331 1
- **Salamandastron** 0 09 914361 5
- **Redwall** 0 09 951200 9
- **Mattimeo** 0 09 967540 4
- **The Pearls of Lutra** 0 09 963871 1

Tales of Redwall by Brian Jacques
Out now in paperback from Red Fox priced £4.99

Redwall Map and Riddler
BRIAN JACQUES

Get ready to take the Redwall Map and Riddler challenge - it's the ultimate Redwall adventure!

The Redwall Map is a perfect reading companion for all fans - old and new - of the legendary Tales of Redwall by Brian Jacques. Beautifully illustrated in full colour, it lavishly charts all the places, landmarks and sites made famous by the Redwall stories.

And there's more!

With the map comes The Redwall Riddler, a quiz book crammed full of riddles to unravel, quick-fire questions, baffling word puzzles and cryptic conundrums. So now you can test your Redwall know-how with tricky brain-teasers like these:

✿ In REDWALL, Cluny the Scourge only has one eye. How is he reputed to have lost the other?

Answer:
✿ In battle with a pike.

Redwall Map and Riddler by Brian Jacques
Red Fox, £4.99 ISBN 0 09 925611 8

JESUS
THE TEENAGE YEARS

by John Farman

'A bookful of belly-laughs' *The Times*

A cheeky but affectionate look at those missing teenage years in Jesus's life. (If you think you've got problems - wait until you read what Jesus had to go through...)

Ever wondered if the Son of God was once a hormonal, zitty, long-haired, angst-ridden young teenage rebel? Do you think Mum nagged him to keep his bedroom tidy? Who were his mates? How did he get on with the oldsters? And just **how** successful was he in the girlfriend department...?!?

Now these and many other mysteries of Jesus's teendom are revealed in this hilariously funny diary of probably the most famous person of all time: Jesus.

JESUS - THE TEENAGE YEARS by John Farman
Red Fox *paperback*, £3.99 ISBN 0 09 955371 6

PART 1

The Very Bloody History of Britain

(WITHOUT THE BORING BITS!)

by John Farman

WARNING!!!

This book could change your ideas about history for ever!

Do you know...

WHO planned the first Channel tunnel?
WHEN 10 Downing Street was built?
WHO invented the television?
WHEN the first Cheddar cheese was made?

Get the low down on life from the heathens to Hitler!
Bizarre, barmy and almost beyond belief, John Farman's
THE VERY BLOODY HISTORY makes boring history
lessons a thing of the - er - past.

John Farman
THE VERY BLOODY HISTORY OF BRITAIN PART 1
Red Fox *paperback*, £3.99   ISBN 0 09 984010 3